Southern Living
Azaleas

By Fred C. Galle
Director of Horticulture
Callaway Gardens, Georgia

Preface

There was never any search to find the author to write this book. America claims no more distinguished horticulturalist than Fred Galle. He has been Director of Horticulture at the celebrated Callaway Gardens in Pine Mountain, Georgia, since 1953, and is the only such director the Gardens has ever known.

A native of Dayton, Ohio, Galle studied Ornamental Horticulture at Ohio State University, receiving a B. S. degree. He served three years in the United States Army in Europe during World War II, and was awarded the Bronze Star and the Purple Heart with one cluster. He then returned to Ohio State to receive his M. S. degree. From 1947 until 1952, he was Assistant Professor of Horticulture at the University of Tennessee where he was also in charge of campus landscape work. During this time he completed most of his course work toward a Ph. D. in Botany and made extensive studies of native azaleas. He returned to Ohio State University as Assistant Professor of Horticulture for one year before going to Callaway Gardens.

Galle is a past President of the American Association of Botanical Gardens and Arboreta, and a past President of the American Horticultural Society. He is a Fellow of the American Association for the Advancement of Science, and a Fellow of the Royal Horticultural Society. He is active in the International Shade Tree Conference, the American Rhododendron Society, the Holly Society of America, as well as a number of other organizations.

Despite his splendid academic background and wide professional commitment, Galle remains a man who would rather dig in the ground than in the archives. He said, "As we do this book, it's important that we be correct in our tables and charts and in all of our information. But we want to express ourselves in honest language that people can understand and respond to. We don't want to try and impress them. We want to help them select the varieties of azaleas that best suit their location, and to guide them into so merging their azaleas in the landscape that they will fit and be beautiful for many generations." In this book he has accomplished just that. Fred Galle has carefully selected his life's knowledge of these beautiful and compelling plants so that you might share it and benefit from it.

Photo Credits

Bellingrath Gardens
Joe Benton
Gerald Crawford
Fred Galle
George Hull

Contents

Introduction

The introduction of azaleas to the South dates back to the mid 1800's when the Southern Indian Hybrid azaleas, or Indicas, were planted by Rev. Drayton at Magnolia Gardens near Charleston, South Carolina in 1848. From this early introduction, the azalea craze spread throughout the Coastal Areas of the Carolinas and the entire South. The more cold hardy Kurume azaleas were first introduced to California in 1915 and, in 1917, to the east by E. H. Wilson, one of America's most enthusiastic plant hunters.

Spring in the South is synonymous with colorful masses of azaleas and native flowering dogwoods, and with their varied and showy display of blooms, azaleas now lead the list of flowering plants for the southern landscape. The flowers of both the evergreen and deciduous azaleas have a remarkable color range: white, yellow, orange, scarlet, crimson, and purple, with many intermediate hues of varying intensity. There are vivid and brilliant shades, pure white, pastel tints, and striped or flecked patterns, as well as solid-colored flowers with or without conspicuous contrasting throats. The attractive five-petaled flowers may appear singly, as hose-in-hose forms or as semidouble and double flowers.

The evergreen azaleas, while prized as individual specimens or in masses for their brilliant splash of color in the spring, contribute also excellent foliage texture and plant form the year round.

The deciduous azaleas, including the ever increasingly popular native azaleas, are important plants for their airy display of colorful flowers. Many of the native species are prized also for their delightful fragrance during the floral season and for their interesting twig and branch formation that accents the winter scene.

The azaleas, noted for their importance to the landscape scene, are also important florists' pot plants, container plants, and hanging basket plants for the patio.

Botanically azaleas are members of the Heath family and, while formerly treated as a separate genus, all are now included in the genus Rhododendron. This is, however, no more confusing than calling our handsome native azaleas "wild honeysuckle". We will leave the problems of classification for later, as we first increase our general appreciation of the azalea.

The Southern gardener is fortunate to have a large selection of hardy evergreen and deciduous azaleas, ranging from dwarf plants to large shrubs adaptable to his own climatic region. One can have azaleas in flower for two months or more with the proper selection of the various cultivars and varieties, an equally important but often overlooked possibility.

Upon meeting the basic and simple cultural requirements, the azalea grows graceful in size and age, thus becoming a prized possession in the Southern garden.

Azaleas in the Landscape

Woodland or naturalized plantings such as this increase in loveliness with the addition of azaleas.

Azaleas, unequaled in beautiful color and profusion of flower, are very popular landscape plants. For many gardeners, the peak of spring is when both the azaleas and dogwoods are in bloom.

It is very important to start with a landscape design or basic plan when selecting azaleas or any plants for the home property. The plan, whether fundamental or very elaborate, should include the elements of design, composition, scale, and texture.

The landscape design should fit the site and the architecture of the home and, most important, should express the interest and personality of the home owner. Gardening, while one of the major leisure forms of recreation, must also vie for time with such sports as golf, boating, and other recreational activities of the home owner. Thus, the garden design should fit into the budget of leisure time, and should not become a maintenance burden. Many plants used in the garden today are high maintenance plants when considering the total time required to prune, fertilize, control pests, and for general seasonal grooming. However, through the proper selection of varieties suitable to the location, azaleas are basically considered low maintenance plants.

A well-planned garden, like a beautiful painting and its effect on the viewer, is the result of careful composition. Throughout the garden there should be a sense of unity; an orderly arrangement of the architectural features and plants in relation to their surroundings.

Scale in the landscape relates to the unity of the planting, tree groups, the land form, and the architectural features. The architectural elements as well as plants should be in scale with one another. Throughout the garden there should be unity and harmony achieved with an understanding of the natural forms, and a repetition or dominance of plant textures.

A garden need not be of large dimensions. It may be a very small terrace, a part of a natural woodland, or it may flow into an open stretch of lawn. A garden should be for enjoyment and a place for retreat, if only for a short time, from the perplexities of the day. A garden of charm has the appearance of being casually refined and well organized, but it is not created without time and effort.

Texture, an important facet of the landscape, is often referred to as the subtle thread running through a well-conceived design. The architectural features such as building walls and walks, all add structural texture to the design, and should complement the overall texture determined by the leaves of the trees and shrubs. The leaves of most evergreen azaleas would be considered as a fine to medium texture in contrast to the leaves of Southern magnolias which are coarse textured.

The seasons of a year bring on many textural and pattern changes. A deciduous azalea or a Japanese maple is admired in the summer for the foliage and in the winter for the prominent form of the twigs and branches. As the new life of spring begins, the form of landscape texture again changes, the soft greens of new leaves add a new dimension.

When azaleas are in full bloom, the texture and composition of the garden may be very bold, and for this reason should be studied carefully. Azaleas can provide some daring color schemes, but it is best to keep one color or color tone dominant over a large area. However, if startling colors are used together, they should be used in color masses rather than individual specimens.

Study the various types of azaleas and note the vast color range. Select varieties that will combine into harmonious color schemes at the time of bloom. White flowers are a good blending agent with the more vivid hues. Separate brilliant colors that may clash with clouds of white azalea varieties or rich evergreen foliage plants. The warm reds and lavenders to purples should be isolated from the hot orange to orange-red shades. It is important, however, to keep in mind the basic principles of landscape design.

Growing plants well is a challenge, but an even greater challenge is to assemble them into a pleasing garden. Check at the library or bookstore for additional reading material on garden design. Also, the advice of an established landscape architect is a good investment because a beautiful garden can be designed that will live for many generations.

One should be able to sense the beauty of a garden during any season. Azalea gardens that are irresistable in the spring should display year-round beauty through a skillful blending of plants and other components of a varied texture. A beautiful landscape is a tasteful blending of the ever changing seasonal forms and textures of plants.

While an azalea enthusiast might wish to use only azaleas and trees in the landscape for a year-round garden, azaleas can be the dominant landscape plant when used in skillful harmony with other plants.

Selecting azaleas to use in the landscape is challenging. Foremost is the selection of species or varieties adaptable to the area. Fortunately, with the large number of species and hybrids from which to choose, one can usually find an azalea to fit the needs and requirements of the site. It is doubtful if any other group of woody plants is so versatile.

When selecting azaleas, think about the season of bloom, the inherent size and form of the

Water line

2"X 12" *rough boards or shingles*

Water will run down the hedge trench on slopes unless it is held back in some way. Soil, shingles, or boards can be used.

For a free-flowing curve:
① lay out curve with hose then stake

spade or sod cutter

② after cutting first side move stakes over 18"

③ Lay hose against stakes and cut other side of trench.

second cut

To lay out a planting trench for a free-flowing curved hedge, use a pliable hose and mark the trench sides as shown.

Be accurate

Chalk line

Planting distances vary according to the plant size and the type of hedge desired. Plants are usually set closer for formal hedges.

plant, the texture and type of foliage, and whether evergreen or deciduous. The discussion of azalea species and hybrids, plus the list of recommended varieties for climatic zones will be a guide and aid in the selection of azalea plants to use. The fun and challenge of gardening is in searching for and trying out new azaleas and other plants to see if they are adaptable to your own garden and your gardening skill.

Azaleas are widely used in the naturalized or informal design and generally require less maintenance. Thus, azaleas are used as foundation plants, in mass borders, as specimens, or in combination with other plants. It is best to discuss briefly each general use separately even though there may be some overlapping or interlocking of use.

Azaleas are often seen in the newly landscaped property as foundation plants (which means the plants used around the home). While there is a need for foundation or base planting, many modern homes today do not require a heavy mass of plants completely around the foundation. In fact, many homes are best viewed with a sparse foundation planting, while mass border plantings are used around or even out in front of the house, or en masse around trees. In selecting azaleas for the foundation planting, carefully choose the flower color to avoid a clash with the color of the building.

With a white or pastel-colored wall, an azalea color other than white should be selected to accent the background. Azaleas with light-colored bloom will be more evident against a dark background. Red brick homes need white, rose, or pink azaleas. Most purple colors clash with the various brick colors unless it's a white or cream-colored brick. The red and salmon, rose and white varieties can be used with the soft pink bricks which are frequently used. Generally, the compact, twiggy evergreen

7

azaleas are used. However, tall plants are needed and even the very dwarf or creeping forms can be used as facing plants in front of larger plants. Deciduous azaleas should also be considered as foundation plantings for the ranch and rustic styled design. The colorful native Florida, Oconee or Flame azalea could be used advantageously around a wood, shingle, or stone and stained wood home. The tracery and shadows of the bare branches in the winter would add interest to the architectural features. Avoid the over use of color in foundation planting. Use only one or two varieties of azaleas, massing the color together.

Remember that azaleas are shade tolerant, however, heavy constant shade or a location on the north side of a building may be too extreme. Avoid the use of tender varieties on windy, exposed corners. Azaleas need good air, drainage, and a location free from "frost pockets". A frequent cause of the failure of azaleas and other plants around the house is the poorly drained backfilled soil and the lime plaster it may contain. Care must be taken to remove all litter and heavy soil which is often left after construction. Correct this condition by grading, using proper soil, and planting in elevated or raised beds to improve the drainage.

All too frequently in many gardens, the azalea dominates only one major burst of color in the spring. However, through the proper selection of varieties or cultivars you can have azaleas in bloom for over two months. Check the recommended list of azaleas for varieties to plant in your climatic area.

Coordinate your selection of colorful azaleas as a painter would, developing pleasing color combinations for the eye and harmonizing with the surroundings.

The strong vivid colors are often over used to the point of being monotonous and overpowering. This can be the case with the vivid red of the Kurume azalea Hinode-giri and the violet red of the Southern Indian azalea Formosa. Consider, too, the architectural features and their colors in the garden when selecting your plants. The violet-red Formosa azalea, a beautiful plant, is often over-used or used in poor color combinations. For example, it is not uncommon to see the violet-red Formosa or the vivid orange-red and red azaleas clashing loudly in disharmony against a brick red building. How much more pleasing this colorful Formosa azalea would be by itself or in combination with the whites or very light pink varieties. The white and light-colored azaleas should be used to soften and blend strong colors. This is very tactfully done by separating the strong colors with white or lighter colors.

It is also important to use azaleas en masse for both their colorful flower effect and plant form. Thus combinations of three to five or more plants of one variety are more pleasing than using five individual strong colors. Careful blending of the same color can be done with several azalea varieties. For example, the following Kurume azaleas might all be used en masse for a pink border: Coral Bells, Pink Pearl, Glory, and Mountain Laurel. These same colors blend well with the salmon pinks of Salmon Beauty and Bridesmaid.

The Kurume azaleas that often clash in color are the vivid reds of Hinode-giri, Himo-crimson and Hershey's Red with the orange-reds of Sherwood Red and Hardy Firefly. These same plants when used alone or in combination with some of the pink varieties or Snow, create a pleasing picture. Similar examples are true of other groups of azaleas. The Southern Indian azaleas, Formosa and Omurasaki with their violet-red colors clash with the orange and reds of Prince of Orange, Pride of Dorking, and President Claeys azaleas.

However, the same varieties of Formosa and Omurasaki blend well with George Lindley Taber, Gulf Pride, Llacina, or the white cultivars or the light pinks such as Lawsal, Pride of Mobile, and others.

Observe established plantings of azaleas in public and home gardens to help you select the varieties that will blend harmoniously by color.

Contrasting colors can be used for special effect, like adding the whipped cream on top of a dessert. Adding one or two white azaleas to a mass of pink or reds gives this effect. Or add a cherry on a topping of cream by using a pink or red azalea in with a mass of white flowered plants. Use care, however, not to over do this "top dressing".

Fortunately, azaleas are easy to transplant and poor color combinations can be marked while the plants are in flower and moved at a later date. Better still, they may be planted while in flower to develop pleasing color combinations, and to eliminate color clashes immediately. In the South, deciduous plants, including azaleas, are often considered secondary to evergreen plants. Unfortunately, with this poor reasoning, the fragrance, beautiful colors, and fall foliage of native azaleas not found in evergreen plants are often overlooked.

Deciduous azaleas should be used in combination with the many fine narrow leaf and broadleaf evergreens available to the gardener. They will add height and twiggy branch formation to the garden scene, not available in the evergreen types. Deciduous azaleas are especially desirable for naturalized or woodland landscape with other indigenous plants.

The evergreen azaleas are also noted for their colorful fall foliage. The foliage on some white azaleas such as Snow is light green in the fall and winter while the foliage of Glacier is a glossy dark green. Many of the pink and red azaleas have orange to reddish fall foliage.

Azaleas are also found in varied plant form. The evergreen azaleas are primarily shrubs ranging from prostrate, creeping forms to medium dense, twiggy shrubs. Others are 6 feet or more, as with the Kurumes or the larger Southern Indian hybrids. The Kaempferi azaleas are usually more upright and open, filling out with age. The Satsuki are often described as dwarfs, but some cultivars may be upright, and even the spreading forms may reach 4 or more feet as they mature. Deciduous azaleas, depending upon the species, can be low shrubs, large shrubs, or even small trees up to 15 or 20 feet in height. It is common to find nurseries advertising dwarf azaleas including such varieties as the Kurume Hinode-giri and even many of the Southern Indian azaleas and others.

Size is relevant. One needs to ask, "Dwarf in relation to what? A giant redwood or a tall pine tree?" Dwarf refers to plants generally 3 feet or less in height after 10 to 15 years of growth. Most Kurume azaleas do not fit this size group but should be included in the medium height group of 5 to 6 feet. Most Satsuki azaleas are included as dwarfs while the Southern Indian azaleas could be considered as medium to large shrubs which are 6 to 8 feet or larger, and large shrubs to small trees, 8 to 15 feet or more.

Thus, the classification of plant habit and height used in this text is as follows:
Ground covers or prostrate forms: 6 to 18 inches
Dwarf shrubs: 18 inches to 3 feet
Satsuki azalea
Medium shrubs: 4 to 6 feet
Kurume azalea
Medium large shrubs: 6 to 8 feet Southern Indian, Kaempferi, Glenn Dales
Large shrubs to small trees: 8 to 15 feet or more, native azaleas

Azaleas are unsurpassed for naturalized plantings and can be used equally well in formal or contemporary designs. Azaleas adapt well to pruning and thus can be used in the formal garden as trimmed hedges or trained specimens. They are even grown as standards, tree form, or used in containers for the patio. Azaleas may even be trimmed in cloud form as in a Japanese or Oriental garden, however, pruned or sculptured plants in this form become high maintenance plants. Attractive hedges of any length and color are possible with azaleas. The hedges can be used in a natural irregular form or closely clipped and trimmed. With Satsuki or Kurume azaleas, a low compact hedge is possible with minimum pruning. For a tall hedge, the medium to large azaleas should be used. A native azalea adapted to the area can be used for a deciduous hedge. It is best to use only one variety or cultivar if uniformity in color, form, and foliage is desired. Freestanding hedges away from individual trees will give a more uniform hedge. Often when trees are used within the hedge for accent, the hedge will show variation in plant growth and height because of competing roots.

Pruning of an azalea hedge should be done in the spring after the plant has finished blooming. Summer growth may also require pinching or pruning back. Pruning will result in a more compact hedge, however, if left unpruned, it will have a naturalized appearance.

Evergreen azaleas may also be used as a screen planting. Many of the Southern Indian or Kaempferi azaleas are excellent for this use. Screen plants may be pruned, but look best if they are left in a more natural state and are used in combination with other plants.

For quick results, plants used for hedges or screens should be planted closer than normal. For example, the following hedge spacing is

The seasonal color and texture changes make this garden a place of interest and charm.

The low, dwarf azalea forms are excellent for formal plantings.

suggested:
Satsuki: 18 to 24 inches apart
Kurumes: 2 to 3 feet apart
Southern Indian Azaleas: 3 to 4 feet apart

Hedge and screen plants can be informally pruned throughout the season. The heaviest pruning should be done after the plant finishes flowering, but no later than August in order to prevent interference with flowering the next season.

Azaleas are most effective when used en masse. Thus, they can add color, form, and fine texture to a border planting. Informal free flowing massed plantings of azaleas around a tree or in a group of trees is very effective. This can be accomplished with different groups of azaleas and the planting can combine medium to large plants with low or dwarf plants as facing plants. Low growing varieties, such as Satsuki, in the foreground backed with taller plants in varied graduation of height, will form a pleasing mass planting.

Azaleas are especially effective when planted near water, especially when both the plant and its reflection can be seen. The source of water can be a pool or pond with individual specimens or groups of plants placed for the added reflections. A pool or pond with land sloping upwards from the water offers numerous possibilities. It is best not to overplant such an area. Instead, leave open areas of grass, or mulched areas. Again, plant the low or dwarf varieties close to the water and back up with the tall plants. In planting near the edge of the water, it may be necessary to use raised mounds to insure drainage.

A woodland or naturalized planting increases in loveliness with the introduction of azaleas. For pleasing results, try to assimilate the use of azaleas in a naturalized area. Plantings of this type may conform to using only native plants. Follow the English style of a wild garden to use both native and introduced plants in a woodland landscape. The style or use will depend on the gardener's taste. Landscaping with only native flora offers a real challenge to retain a natural beauty.

The dark green foliage of tall evergreens such as pines, spruce, or hemlocks is an excellent background for azaleas. The fine textured foliage of a conifer, or the larger and coarser texture of the many broadleaf evergreens gives a good effect. The azaleas thus will serve as a background for the numerous small herbaceous plants adaptable for a woodland garden. The skillful placement of azaleas in a woodland scene requires study of the entire area. They may outline the garden path, be tastefully placed with a background of other plants, or come into view around a turn. The gardener who can grow azaleas in his area is fortunate because a well-designed garden with the colorful placement of azaleas will offer years of beauty.

For selecting plants to use with your azaleas, please refer to the chapter on companion plants.

Planting and care of Azaleas

Before buying new azalea plants, consider the basic cultural requirements of the plant. Understanding these cultural needs of the azalea will pay dividends in developing the plants into healthy and handsome specimens.

The fundamental requirements include:

1. Garden site, climatic zone, and exposure.
2. Soil: aeration, acidity, pH, organic matter, and mycorrhiza.
3. Planting techniques: depth, drainage, spacing, and mulching.
4. Fertilizer.
5. Pruning.

Following the cultural requirements of garden site, soil, and planting is extremely important before purchasing the quality azalea plant that is adapted to your area. In all good plant growth, the cultural requirements interact and contribute to the overall success. Following the old adage "Plant a 50 cent plant in a $5.00 hole" is still sound advice. Spending the extra time and effort to satisfy the basic cultural requirements will result in the plant's responding tenfold.

The large evergreen leaved rhododendrons and other members of the Heath family have the same general cultural requirements as azaleas and can be adapted to these plants.

For success in your azalea garden, select a suitable site. Soil should not be heavy clay or pure sand because azaleas grow the best in well-drained, open, acid, humus soil. The site should be free of "frost pockets". High open shade is preferred to a full open area. Light shade for azaleas is necessary for the lower South, Zones 8 and 9. Morning sun is preferable to noon or afternoon sun. Late flowering azaleas do best with protection from the intense midafternoon exposure to the sun. Pine trees provide a light-filtered shade while deciduous trees such as oaks and sweet gums

This is an example of fertilizer injury.

This is the result of deep planting.

12

should be trimmed high to allow sunlight to filter through. Plants should also be given protection from exposure to high winds through the use of trees or a screen planting on the windward side. Avoid planting azaleas near shallow rooted trees, such as silver maple and elms, because of the competition of the roots for moisture and nutrients. It has often been observed that tender azaleas are more adaptable in a shady northern exposure than the same plants receiving winter sun.

Use plants adaptable to your plant hardiness zone. The plant hardiness zone map was prepared by the United States National Arboretum in cooperation with the American Horticulture Society. A large color map is available as Miscellaneous Publication No. 814 from the Superintendent of Documents, United States Government Printing Office, Washington, D.C. The 10 temperature zones represent a 10° F. range of average annual maximum temperatures. Each zone is divided into subzones "a" and "b", showing a 5°F. division.

There are plant hardiness maps from several sources, however, reference to hardiness zones in this book refers to the U.S.D.A. Plant Hardiness Zone Map #814. A copy of this map is presented in this book, along with a range of average annual minimum temperatures.

Zone 1	-50°
Zone 2	-50° to -40°
Zone 3	-40° to -30°
Zone 4	-30° to -20°
Zone 5	-20° to -10°
Zone 6a	-10° to -5°
Zone 6b	-5° to 0°
Zone 7a	0° to +5°
Zone 7b	+5° to +10°
Zone 8a	+10° to +15°
Zone 8b	+15° to +20°
Zone 9a	+20° to +25°
Zone 9b	+25° to +30°
Zone 10a	+30° to +35°
Zone 10b	+35° to +40°

The zone rating is an important guide for cold hardiness of particular plants and indicates how far north it might safely be planted. It is equally important to know how far south a plant will survive, and we have been concerned for many years about adding the range in which a plant will grow to the hardiness rating. Unfortunately, this information is not as readily available. However, we shall give the range of a plant's adaptablility when it is known.

A hardiness map, unfortunately, cannot list all of the local variations or microclimatic areas. It is often found that a city temperature may be several degrees warmer than the surrounding countryside. Likewise, the city area might also have a higher pollution index than the surrounding areas.

SOILS
Soil for azaleas should be in good physical structure, open and friable to provide drainage, and acid with sufficient quantities of organic matter to retain moisture. Most soils throughout the South are acid and can be made suitable for azaleas with the addition of organic matter. Heavy clay soils or pure sand can be improved by the addition of organic matter such as peat, leaf mold, or pine bark. Clay soils can often be improved by adding sand to the organic matter to provide good drainage.

An added note of precaution: frequently mortar or lime is found around the foundation of brick or stone homes. This soil and debris should be removed and replaced with new woodsy loam soil.

SOIL ACIDITY
The acidity or alkalinity of a soil is based on the hydrogen ion concentration expressed as

pH. The pH scale is graduated from 0 to 14. A pH of 7.0 is neutral; reactions above 7.0 are alkaline, and below 7.0, the reactions are acid. The degree of alkalinity or acidity increases or decreases by 10 times the previous level for each whole number change. Thus, a pH of 8.0 is 10 times more alkaline than a pH 7.0, and it is 100 times more alkaline than a pH of 6.0.

Most soils throughout the South are acid and are suitable for azaleas unless the soil has been previously limed for agronomic crops. A soil analysis, however, is the only way to determine soil pH. Soil testing kits are available, but often the results can be sporadic, due to the deterioration of the chemical reagents. Your County Agent can provide information on how to get your soil tested for pH and nutrients. The soil test report will indicate if lime or acid forming materials are needed to adjust the pH of your soil. The County Agent's office is often located in or near your county courthouse.

While azaleas grow in a wide range of acidity, the best range is between pH 5.0 to 6.0. Azaleas growing in a low of pH of 3.5 to 4.5 will be healthy, but they will grow at a slower rate than normal. Azaleas growing in a soil pH of 6.5 and above may appear yellow, an indication of chlorosis. To increase the acidity of soils above pH 6.0, the addition of ground sulfur (not aluminum sulfate) is recommended. Approximately 1.5 pounds of ground sulfur per 100 square feet, mixed into the soil will lower the pH from 6.0 to 5.5, or ½ point. Sandy soil will require less sulfur, 0.5 pound per 100 square feet, while heavy clay soils will require up to 2.5 pounds of sulfur plus the addition of organic matter to the clay. It is also advisable to add ½ pound of ferrous sulfate with the sulfur per each 100 square feet of soil.

The relationship between soil pH and the availability of iron is important to azaleas. Iron is available to plants in an acid soil of pH 5.0 to 6.0. Azaleas deficient in iron show signs of

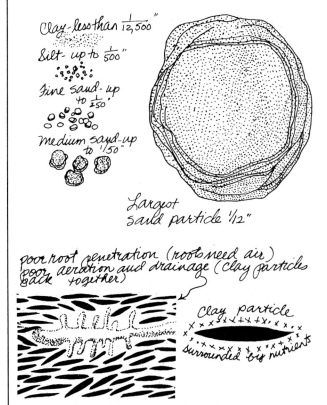

Clay- less than 1/12,500"

Silt- up to 1/500"

Fine sand- up to 1/250"

Medium sand- up to 1/50"

Largest sand particle 1/12"

poor root penetration (roots need air) poor aeration and drainage (clay particles pack together)

Clay particle surrounded by nutrients

When a clay soil gets wet, it dries slowly because movement of water down through the soil is obstructed and the circulation of air within the soil is seriously hampered. The result is severely inhibited root growth.

sand particle

In a sandy soil, the rounded and irregular sand particles rest against one another, and there are air spaces between the particles. The result is excellent aeration and very free drainage, and therefore, the soil dries rapidly. Because of the frequent watering required, nutrients leach away quickly and the soil therefore needs feeding at frequent intervals.

iron chlorosis: the leaves are yellow with prominent dark green veins.

Chlorosis may be caused by other factors however, such as poor root growth, over fertilization, soil nematodes, or poorly drained soils. If the plant is suffering from iron chlorosis, quick, but temporary results can be obtained by spraying the foliage with iron sulfate (ferrous sulphate or copperas) at the rate of 1 ounce per every 2 gallons of water. Cheleated iron or iron sequestrenes are also effective as a foliage spray for iron chlorosis.

A plant deficient in magnesium looks very similar in the early stages to iron chlorosis. The yellowish leaves later develop reddish-purple blotches, followed by a browning of the tip and margin. Epsom salts (magnesium sulfate is a source of magnesium) can be applied as a foliage spray at the rate of 1 ounce per gallon of water.

ORGANIC MATTER
Azaleas respond directly to the amount of organic matter added to the soil. Humus is the end product of the decomposition of organic matter. Humus soils are light and open, thus improving the soil aeration. It increases the soil's water holding capacity and reduces the leaching out of soil nutrients. Humus aids in maintaining an acid soil and adds nutrients to the plant.

Organic matter in the form of humus in the soil or as a mulch around the plant is important for good azalea growth. Organic matter for the soil is available in a variety of sources. Leaf mold, shredded and partly decomposed leaves of hardwoods and conifers, such as oaks and pines, is an excellent source. Coarse sphagnum peat moss has been a very popular soil amendment. Native sedge peat moss is generally of a finer texture and not as good as the imported sphagnum peat moss. Many nurserymen today, however, are replacing peat

moss with ground pine bark. We have used ground pine bark for over 10 years as a source of organic matter and found it very good. Pine bark is a by-product of the lumber industry and is available in different grades. One grade is similar to a coarse peat and is ideal as a soil amendment. Coarser grades are more important as a mulch.

The use of sawdust is also being replaced by pine bark. During the decomposition of sawdust, nitrogen is removed from the soil and must be replaced. Additional nitrogen can be added at the rate of approximately $\frac{1}{4}$ pound of ammonium sulfate (20% N) or $\frac{1}{4}$ pound of ammonium nitrate (33% N) per bushel of sawdust. Add organic matter at the rate of $\frac{1}{3}$ to $\frac{1}{2}$ by volume to both sandy or clay soil. Mix the soil and organic material throughly before planting.

Mycorrhiza is a soil fungi associated with the roots of ericaceous plants. Mycorrizal fungi aids the roots in the absorption of nutrients and water in a mutual or symbiotic relationship. New soils can be inoculated with mycorrhizal fungi by adding soil from areas of native azaleas or soil from an established azalea garden. Soil acidity, humus, and moisture are essential for mycorrhizae. Thus, mulches also play an important role with mycorrhiza in replenishing humus to the soil as it decays.

PLANTS AND PLANTING
Study the site for your azaleas, checking for exposure to winds, soil type, and good drainage. Again, it is advisable to have the soil tested for pH and to make adjustments, if necessary. For mass planting, prepare the entire area or bed by rototilling the area, working in sufficient organic matter such as acid peat, shredded pine bark, or leaf mold. Good soil preparation is essential for plant growth — 4 to 6 inches of organic matter worked thoroughly into the average garden soil is important. Azaleas are easy to transplant and

can be moved at any season of the year if proper care is given. Early spring is ideal in most areas, but the plants can be moved while in full flower, or in the fall or early winter.

The best source of good azaleas is reliable nurserymen or garden centers specializing in azaleas. Unfortunately, in many areas this is not possible and you must rely on the local garden center. The average garden center is not, however, a nursery or a grower of plants, but a retailer obtaining his plants from wholesale nurseries. Buy only top quality plants. Misshaped plants, plants with weak growth and poor foliage color, and plants usually sold at discount prices are no bargains. Be sure that the plant you purchase is adapted to your area. Frequently the term "suitable for planting" is used in sale ads. A broomstick or a dead plant could be "suitable for planting", but the question in point is whether the plant is healthy, hardy, and adapted to your area.

Large balled and burlapped plants — B & B — are being replaced by container plants in 1, 3, and 5 gallon sizes. Buy quality compact plants, avoiding the open, leggy, poorly grown plants. Select plants in flower for color combination, however, container grown plants offer the opportunity to obtain named varieties or cultivars at any season of the year. Container grown plants, however, are generally root-bound and the roots should be broken or washed out, to insure that they will develop in the new planting soil. This can be done by cutting the root mass with a sharp knife from top to bottom. Failure to loosen the tightly bound roots will often result in very weak or dead plants within the first year.

When digging holes, be sure to check on soil drainage. "Remember the $5.00 hole." The average hole for a 2-gallon container plant should be approximately 24 inches across and a minimum of 12 inches deep. Be sure to add and mix organic matter at the rate of ⅓ to ½

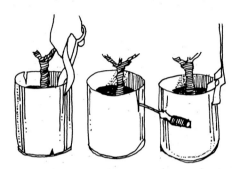

Cut cans with tin shears, a notched screwdriver, or a manufactured cutter. Be careful of sharp edges.

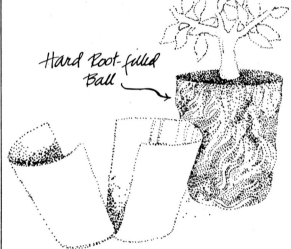

Hard Root-filled Ball

If roots are so crowded that you can't break them out of the root ball, the plant will have trouble and may not survive.

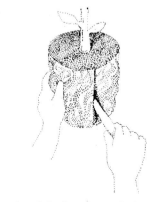

Loosen roots of the hard root ball with a knife or pointed stick.

*Azaleas define the walkway
and stream.*

Azaleas are excellent as container plants, and are particularly effective in hanging baskets.

Azaleas are used here to screen a drive-way.

The azaleas form a low hedge for foreground interest, and are used well with the dogwood.

Here the azaleas create a surrounding for the terrace.

The azaleas covering the slope form a transition between the woods and the streamside plantings.

*The container plants are used to create
a line on the edge of the terrace.*

*This is one of the more effective uses
of the larger azalea specimens.*

*The azaleas form a frame for the entry
to the terrace.*

The native deciduous azaleas are particularly effective for creating a natural woodland setting.

The azaleas and the dogwood are combined well in an informal mass planting.

Native azaleas are excellent for planting under a canopy of large trees.

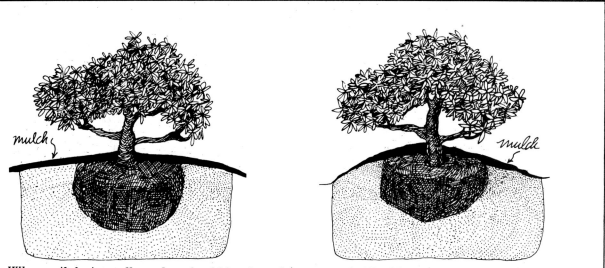

Where soil drains well, azaleas should be planted in prepared soil with root crowns several inches above grade. In heavy soils, azaleas may be planted considerably higher and then mulched well.

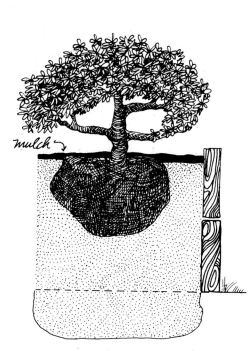

Raised beds 18 inches above the soil grade are good where alkaline water and heavy soil are problems.

by volume to the transplanting soil, or to the soil that is backfilled around the plant.

A common fault in transplanting azaleas is planting too deep. The top of the root ball or root mass of a container plant should be at the surface of the ground or slightly higher. Remember, this is contradictory advice for most plants. Except for sandy, well-drained soil, shallow planting for azaleas is advisable. Be sure to firm the base of the planting hole. If this soil is left loose and fluffy, it will compress after planting, allowing the plant to sink deep into the hole.

In heavy clay soils that may become water-logged, it is advisable to plant at least half out of the ground or in extreme cases, entirely above ground. The raised beds may be confined by logs or rocks and will require increased maintenance, including watering during the summer. On large individual plants it is often advisable to make a dish-like depression around the plant to retain water. For mass or bed planting, and often for small plants, this depression is not necessary if proper soil preparation and transplanting techniques are followed.

On large areas the soil drainage can be improved by establishing a 4-inch clay drain tile or plastic drain pipe at least 18 to 24 inches below the surface. The drains may be as close as 10 feet apart, and a maximum of 20 to 25 feet apart. The drain tile should have sufficient fall and be laid on a bed of sand and gravel covered with at least 6 to 12 inches of gravel. Fiberglass matting is excellent to use to cover the joints of the tile. For more detailed information on establishing soil drainage, contact the State Extension Agricultural Engineer through your local County Agent.

Deciduous native azaleas are also becoming available in containers. Move native azaleas from the woods during the dormant season, late fall, winter, or early spring. Many states now have laws which prohibit the collection of native plants, so know the laws and regulations in your own area and obtain permission from the landowner before collecting any plants. Many gardeners are fortunate to have native azaleas on their own properties and need only to move them to a more desirable area within the landscape planting. Native azalea plants usually have poor root systems, often widely spread and sparse. It is best to move small plants because they can withstand the shock of transplanting. Dig carefully to obtain as many roots as possible. After digging, the plant should be severely pruned to within 6 to 8 inches from the ground. Cutting back the top is most important to balance the very poor root system normally found with native azaleas. Cut back plants generally will produce flower buds after the second season.

Spacing of plants offers several possibilities. If an immediate effect is desired, close spacing of small plants is required. Spacing with the future development of a plant in mind may look very open and sparse for several years. The best procedure is to space close at first and then transplant as the plants develop. The latter method, especially for new homeowners,

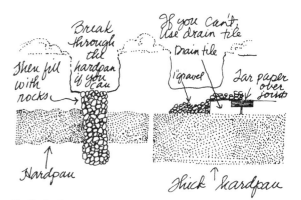

Soil drainage may be poor even if the surface drainage is excellent. A rock-filled drain hole works effectively only when it goes through to a layer of soil that drains water rapidly.

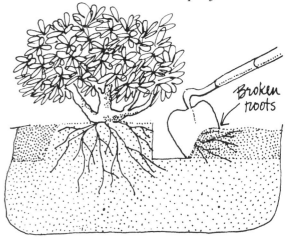

This is the wrong way to cultivate around azaleas. Cultivate shallowly where there is a danger of cutting or exposing roots.

offers the best solution since azaleas are very easy to transplant.

The following is a guide for general spacing of several groups of azaleas:

Kurume and Satsuki Azaleas: 3 to 4 feet minimum; for full development, 4 to 6 feet apart.

Southern Indian Azaleas: 4 to 6 feet minimum; for full development, 6 to 8 feet apart.

Beltsville Dwarfs: 18 to 24 inches.

18

For close spacing and an immediate effect, place the azaleas even closer than suggested above, and then transplant as the plants develop.

Hedges of azaleas are planted close and the following spacing is suggested:
    Kurume and Satsuki hybrids: 2 to 3 feet.
    Southern Indian hybrids: 3 to 4 feet.

WATER AND MULCH
The newly transplanted azaleas should be watered well before applying the mulch. This provides another opportunity to be sure the azaleas are not planted too deep. If the plant sinks down, it is too deep and should be replanted higher. In most areas, the new plants will require additional watering during dry periods because azaleas are shallow rooted and may dry out during periods of drought. Throughout the South we often have long periods of drought – these frequently occur in May and again in late August, September, and October. Properly mulched plants may only require weekly watering, if sufficient rainfall of ½ to 1 inch has not occurred during the week. Plants should not go into the dormant winter season in a desiccated or dry condition.

Mulching of new plants is very important because it aids in conserving soil moisture. Within different areas of the country there are numerous good mulching materials. Some of these materials are also used as sources of organic matter and were discussed previously. Shredded hardwood leaves and leaf mold are frequently available. Pine needles and shredded pine bark are both excellent. Other materials include ground corncobs, peanut hulls, pecan shells, bagasse, cotton waste, wood chips, and shingletow. A good mulch should be thick, but loose and airy. Peat moss and sawdust are not desirable mulching materials unless they are used with other coarser materials because they frequently form a surface crust when dry and often shed water.

Unground fallen leaves of hardwood trees and many broadleaf evergreens, such as Southern magnolia, holly, and others, will also pack very tightly and will shed water until they have been broken down or rotted.

The mulch should be at least 3 inches deep. Organic mulches decompose, adding humus to the soil and aiding in keeping a soil acid. Due to this continual decomposition, organic mulch must be renewed at least annually.

Remember, good mulches are essential because in addition to conserving soil moisture they:
    (1) reduce the freezing of soils in the winter,
    (2) increase water penetration and reduce run-off of rain,
    (3) keep the soil aerated,
    (4) encourage biological action such as mycorrhizae in the soil,
    (5) aid in keeping down weeds, and
    (6) eliminate the need for cultivation.

Azaleas, due to their shallow root system, should not be cultivated with hand tools. Weeds coming through a mulch are easily controlled by hand pulling or spot treating with a chemical.

FERTILIZER
A soil high in organic matter, along with the use of an organic mulch, is more important to good azalea growth than fertilizer. Fertilizer is often regarded as the panacea for all plant problems, but it is not a cure-all. Healthy azaleas, however, do respond to low or moderate applications of fertilizer.

Plants do require a number of different chemical substances, and 16 elements are generally considered essential for plant life. The three most important elements are nitrogen, phosphorus, and potassium. These three elements are present in every balanced fertilizer and are marked on the bag by the numbers "10-6-4", "8-8-8", or "12-6-6".

The first number shows the percentage of nitrogen; the second, the percentage of phosphorus as P_2O_5 and the third, the percentage of potassium as K_2O. Each of these three major elements is important for plant growth.

Nitrogen is essential for vegetative growth. Dark green foliage is an indicator of ample nitrogen. Excessive nitrogen, however, can prevent flowering and increase pest problems. Plants lacking in nitrogen have yellow foliage and indicate poor growth.

Phosphorus assists in maturing plants and in flower bud initiation.

Potassium (potash) is important in the formation of starch and sugar, and in the development of leaves, branches, and flowers.

Iron is one of the most important micronutrients for azaleas and is included in many balanced fertilizers, or it can be applied as a special product, as discussed earlier in its relationship to pH.

Only periodic soil tests, at least annually, can serve as a true guide to the type and quantity of fertilizer to add. More azaleas are killed by over fertilizing than through the lack of fertilizer. Small amounts of fertilizer applied at frequent intervals during the active growing season are best. A general recommendation is to fertilize when new growth starts, or after flowering of the Kurume azaleas. Some growers prefer one to three (or monthly) applications up to July 15. In the deep South, light applications can continue through August.

There are both special azalea fertilizers of varying analyses and all-purpose fertilizers, such as 8-8-8 or cottonseed meal, 7-3-2. Many nurserymen are using a 12-6-6 fertilizer with approximately 70% of the nitrogen in a slow release form. This particular formulation has

Azaleas have growth buds in the leaf axiles along the stem. Thus, new growth will originate close to any cut you make.

Growth buds in leaf axils.
Pinch terminal bud to induce branching.

Repeat pinching process on new branches formed earlier.

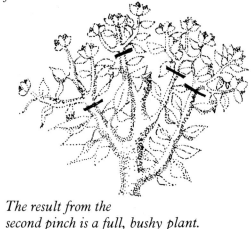

The result from the second pinch is a full, bushy plant.

Sometimes the removal of a terminal bud creates a problem . . .

If you cut runaways like these . . .

the buds below the cut may respond like this.

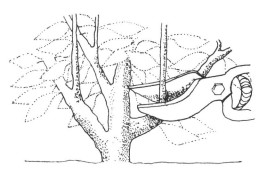

Frequently, it is best to cut such runaways off at the base.

Poor sanitation adversely affects rooting percentage.

This illustrates the effect of pH: The soil pH on the left was 7.4, and on the right it was 5.9.

been important for container grown plants requiring frequent watering. Only one application is generally applied in early spring, and occasionally a light second application in July. A systemic pesticide for the control of lace bug can be applied separately, but it saves time to apply it with the fertilizer. As a safety precaution when handling all fertilizers, use a pair of lightweight disposable gloves for the hands.

Apply approximately ½ to 1 pound (½ to 1 pint) of fertilizer (12-6-6 or 10-5-7) per 100 square feet of bed space. Do not apply fertilizer close to the stem of the plant, but do scatter the fertilizer evenly on the mulch. For a small 12-inch plant, 1 teaspoonful of fertilizer per plant is ample. Large individual plants may require up to 1 tablespoon per foot in height. Cottonseed meal, where available, is a good organic fertilizer, and due to its lower analysis (7-3-2), may be used at a slightly higher rate. After fertilizing, water the plants well.

Extra nitrogen is often required since it is very soluble and is often used by bacteria in decaying organic matter, such as sawdust, becoming temporarily unavailable to the plant. Ericaceous plants like azaleas do not respond well to nitrate fertilizer. Ammonium sulfate (20% N) or ureaform nitrogen (38% N) are recommended materials. If sawdust is used as a source of organic matter or mulch, use ¼ pound ammonium sulfate per bushel of material and apply at least two or three monthly applications at the same rate.

Liquid fertilizers and special fertilizer material, such as Osmocote, are often used by experienced growers. Container grown plants, due to increased watering and leaching are often given more frequent, but light, application of fertilizer throughout the growing season.

Placing a cork in the drain hole makes thorough watering possible without moving the basket. Remove cork after watering to allow proper drainage.

Add a light mulch and scratch soil surface around edge of container with a hand cultivator, screwdriver, or sharp stick, and then soak with water until root ball is saturated.

Soak the root ball instead of watering the foliage which deflects water away from the container.

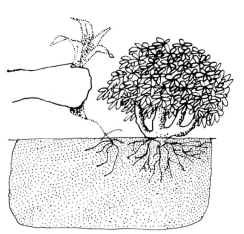

This is the right way to cultivate around azaleas. Hand-pull weeds growing close to the plants— pull up and away.

Carefully pull weeds up and away from plants. Roots may be entwined and you may pull out both plants.

PRUNING

Azaleas generally require very little pruning, except for removing deadwood, and shaping, and developing into compact plants. Small plants should be pruned to develop a compact branching system. Tall, leggy plants can be severely cut back to rejuvenate. The best season to prune is after flowering and before flower buds are formed in mid-summer. Late summer and fall pruning will often result in fewer flowers in the next season. Old plants often become open and irregular in shape with long, strong vigorous branches. These heavy canes should be cut back within the body of the plant and often to the ground. Old plants can also be rejuvenated by cutting back to within 6 to 8 inches from the ground. Strong new basal shoots will develop and these may often require pinching to induce additional branching.

Several new chemicals are used by commercial azalea growers for chemical pruning. These chemicals are applied to new growth and require exact amounts. The treated plants must be watered in 10 to 15 minutes to stop extensive damage. Other growth retardant chemicals, such as Cycocel or B-Nine are used as an aid to developing compact plants and to increase flower bud formations. Both of these two types of chemicals (the chemical pruner and the retardant) are not recommended for the homeowner, except for experimental use and the manufacturer's recommendations should be closely followed. The general advice for azalea pruning is frequent but light to moderate pinching during the spring season to develop and shape the plant.

Nitrogen deficiency causes leaf drop, foliage discoloration, and poor growth.

The roots of root-bound plants like this one should be broken or washed out to insure that they will develop in the new planting soil.

Azaleas deficient in iron like this plant show signs of iron chlorosis: The leaves are yellow with prominent dark green veins.

These are cut back native azaleas that were heeled in sawdust for 1 season before planting in a permanent location.

24

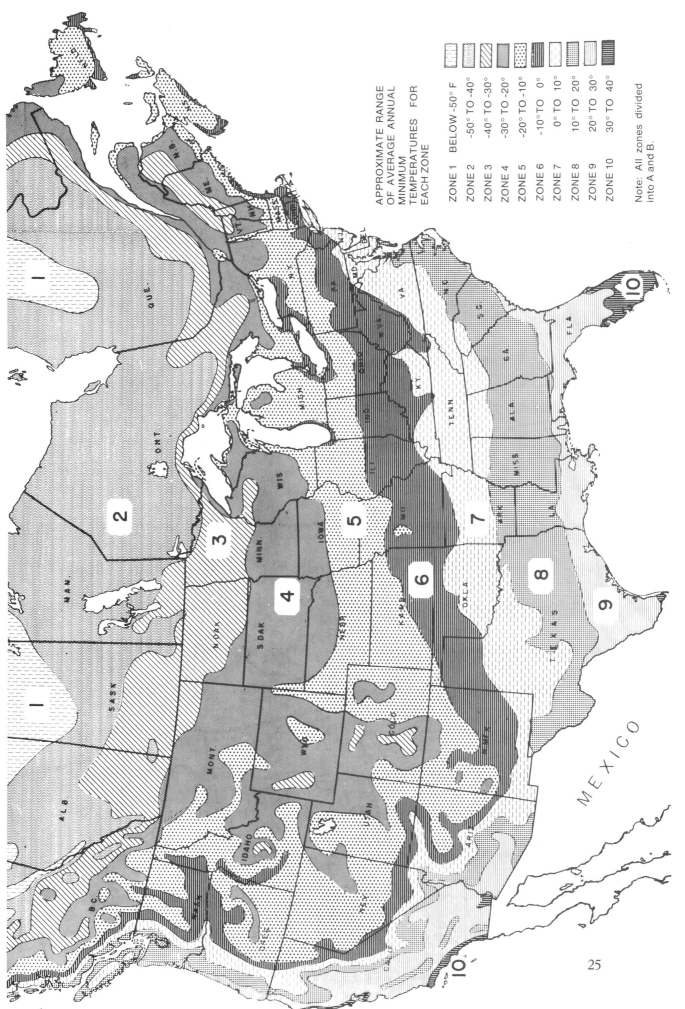

APPROXIMATE RANGE
OF AVERAGE ANNUAL
MINIMUM
TEMPERATURES FOR
EACH ZONE

ZONE 1 BELOW -50° F
ZONE 2 -50° TO -40°
ZONE 3 -40° TO -30°
ZONE 4 -30° TO -20°
ZONE 5 -20° TO -10°
ZONE 6 -10° TO 0°
ZONE 7 0° TO 10°
ZONE 8 10° TO 20°
ZONE 9 20° TO 30°
ZONE 10 30° TO 40°

Note: All zones divided
into A and B.

Special Azalea Culture

Azaleas make excellent pot or container plants for outdoors or in the house. Azaleas are now standard pot plants, flowered from mid-December through May, and in some areas they are flowered the year round. While all azaleas can be forced to flower out of season, the evergreen types are generally used because of the added feature of handsome foliage. The types used by the florist are the Kurume, Pericat, Belgian Indian, and Rutherford hybrids. The standard forcing varieties used commercially include Coral Bells, Snow, and Pink Pearl among the Kurumes; Madam Pericat, Dawn, and Sweetheart Supreme among the Pericats; Alaska, Albert-Elizabeth, Paul Schaeme, Dorothy Gish, Gloria, Mission Bells, Road Runner, Snowbank or Cherokee White, Dogwood, Pink Ruffles, Easter Parade, and Redwings among the Belgian and Rutherford hybrids. It is not necessary to be limited to the standard florist varieties since the varieties from the various groups discussed in Chapter 7 can also be used. The Glenn Dale and Satsuki hybrids are good forcing varieties, but they are seldom used commercially. The Satsuki hybrids and some late flowering varieties of the Glenn Dales, however, are difficult to force early in the winter season.

A basic understanding on the care of a forced azalea and a brief knowledge of how these plants are handled commercially will aid the home gardener.

Upon receiving a potted azalea, check the pot to see if the plant needs water. If so, water it thoroughly before displaying it in your home. The plant should be kept in a well-lighted room of 65°F. or cooler. At normal room temperatures of 72° to 75°F. the flowers will last only a short time. Due to the low humidity in the average homes, the foliage should be syringed lightly every day, and the pot watered when needed. A gravel-filled tray or saucer beneath the potted plant will assist in keeping a moist humidity around the plant. You may also wish to try the automatic watering or wick pots now available for house plants. After flowering, the potted azalea must be kept indoors until frost-free weather in the spring. Some commercial varieties of potted azalea may be of a variety suitable for outdoor use, but because it is in active growth, it must be kept indoors until there is frost-free weather before planting out in the garden. Move the plant, if possible to a cool room of 50° to 55°F., keeping the pot moist and continuing to syringe the foliage. You may find it necessary to pinch or prune the new growth as it develops to maintain a compact plant. Tender azalea varieties will have to remain as a pot or container plant or be discarded as we frequently do with many holiday plants.

Commercially, the Christmas holiday azalea requires from five to six weeks of cool 45° to 50°F. temperature before being forced into flower. This is done in cold storage rooms, and the plants are kept moist. To prevent leaf drop, the plants are lighted for 12 hours each day with 100 watt bulbs spaced 4 feet apart and 2 feet above the plants. Following the cool storage, the plants are moved to a greenhouse at 55° to 60°F. and forced into flower in three to five weeks. During the forcing, the azalea foliage is syringed frequently and the plants are kept watered after the root growth has started. Light applications of a liquid fertilizer are also applied during the forcing period. Some azalea varieties may require longer cool storage treatments and even a longer forcing period. Refrigerated storage is required to hold azaleas for later spring and summer forcing. Prior to this last stage of cool storage and forcing, the plants have two to four years of intensive outdoor culture, developing into healthy well-shaped plants. Hopefully, this brief discussion will increase the appreciation for gift plants.

The azalea enthusiast without a greenhouse but with a cool 60° to 65°F. room can also force azaleas indoors. This normally will require

The dwarf, spreading habit of this azalea is very suitable for hanging baskets.

Constant pruning of this espalier is required to maintain the decorative effect of the trellis.

using the hardy varieties of the area. The plants should be established in containers and kept outdoors for the cold treatment. A hardy azalea variety in a container may freeze unless given protection, but will be perfectly hardy established in the garden.

Keep the container plants in a wind-free area and mulch heavily with pine straw or shredded bark around the containers. Outdoors, the potted plant can also be plunged into soil up to the pot rim and then mulched. Maintain a good watering program since container and potted plants will dry out faster than established garden plants. A light cover of pine straw on the foliage or a cover of plastic wrap above the foliage will give the plant protection from a light frost. Some growers may even wish to try the tender varieties, such as Belgian and Rutherford hybrids, giving protection outdoors and bringing them indoors before the heavy cold winter sets in. These varieties often will withstand a light freeze, but the container plant should not be exposed to temperatures below 25°F. In some areas of Zones 7b and 8, the container plants can often be left outdoors until late December before bringing them in to be forced. The forced azalea should not be moved outdoors again until frost-free weather in the spring.

Select the containers for azaleas to enhance the plant. Since azaleas are shallow rooted, it is not necessary to use the standard clay pots or wood containers. An 18-inch azalea will be more attractive in a container 6 to 10 inches deep instead of a standard 12- to 14-inch size. The container should not detract from the plant and should be selected for its shape, texture, and color. Many attractive plant containers are available today, or you can even design and make your own from wood or other materials. Wood containers should be treated with a clear or natural green copper naphanate wood preservative. The penta or PCP wood preservatives are toxic to plants and should not be

27

used. An azalea pot or fern pot is ¾ as high as it is wide, thus an 8-inch pot is only 6 inches high as compared to a standard 8- x 8-inch pot.

The glazed and non-glazed clay pots are ideal containers. The glazed pots, due to their non-porous surface, will require less watering in warmer weather than the porous container. A regular clay pot can be slipped inside a large attractive glazed pot for display.

The hanging basket container or pot should also be selected to enhance the plant. While the wood and clay containers are most popular, containers are also available in metal, concrete, and plastic. The container should have drainage holes to prevent the plant from becoming waterlogged. Depending upon the type of container, each will require different watering techniques at different intervals.

For container culture, a good, well-drained organic soil mixture should be used, such as ½ organic matter from coarse sphagnum peat or shredded pine bark and ½ coarse sand. Be sure to cover the drainage holes with broken pottery or a piece of metal or plastic screen. A light layer of medium gravel in the bottom of the container should be added to insure good drainage.

Container plants will require more care and maintenance than established plants in the garden, particularly in watering and feeding. The plants are subject to the same insects and diseases as the garden plant.

As the container plants grow, they will require frequent to daily watering which will increase during the warm weather as the plant grows and because of increased evaporation. As watering is increased, the leaching and loss of nutrients from the soil medium also increases. Heavy watering rather than light watering is far more important and reduces the problem of harmful soluble salts that may cause damage to the roots.

Liquid fertilizers are recommended. Use a commercial soluble preparation as directed, or make your own by mixing 2 to 4 teaspoons of a complete acid fertilizer per gallon of water. Apply the liquid fertilizer every two to three weeks during the active growing season, reducing the amount in the late summer and fall as the plants go into their dormant season.

Azalea plants in containers will require annual pruning and pinching to maintain a desirable shape. Prune after flowering and pinch back new growth during the growing season if a compact plant is desired.

After one or two years, most container plants are likely to become root-bound, and therefore will need repotting with fresh potting soil. After removing the plant from the pot, if the roots are matted on the outside of the root ball, repotting is necessary. It is not necessary, however, for annual repotting to a larger container unless desired. Some of the outer roots should be cut from top to bottom, and some of the soil can be washed free of the root ball. In repotting, use an organic soil mixture as previously described; firm the soil mixture and thoroughly water after repotting. Avoid replanting too deeply in the container. Most repotting should be done after the plant finishes flowering, or in the spring when the plant is moved outdoors.

The type of azalea used in a container is generally less important than the care and maintenance of the plant. Of course, a colorful, hardy variety is important, but proper maintenance is required year round to have a healthy and beautiful container plant.

Azaleas suitable for hanging baskets should have a dwarf, spreading habit rather than tall vigorous growth. The Belgian, Rutherford, and Satsuki hybrids are all good basket plants, as are the spreading and pendulous types.

BONSAI

Azaleas are highly prized for bonsai or "tray trees". The dwarf evergreen azaleas such as the Kurume and Satsuki hybrids with their small foliage are readily adaptable. The Beltsville dwarf azlaeas, as they become better known, should prove to be excellent bonsai material. Of the azalea species, both *Rhododendron kiusianum* and *Rhododendron serpyllifolium* are prized in Japan and in this country for their use as bonsai subjects.

Bonsai is a special facet of indoor-outdoor container growing, with the emphasis on the art of pruning and training in the bonsai fashion. A budding bonsai enthusiast will benefit by reading one or more of the excellent books available on the subject, and by studying the pictures of prized bonsai specimens. It may also be beneficial to join one of the many bonsai clubs available throughout the country.

It is a mistake to think that the dwarfing of bonsai is from poor soil and starvation because a humus, sandy, well-drained soil is necessary, and constant care in watering with a modest fertilization program is essential. Dwarfing of the plants is done by articulate pruning of the top growth and at least annual repotting and root pruning. The shallow and often gnarled root system of azaleas are added features of the bonsai as well as the trunk and branching habit. The bending and wiring of branches to create special effects is usually done in the spring.

The art and care of bonsai is a rapidly expanding new interest for gardeners, but it requires attention twelve months a year.

The azalea bonsai should be kept in a shady location during the growing season, and in the winter it should be moved to a cool greenhouse or a frost-free pit or cold frame. Repotting and pruning is generally done after flowering. The pinching of new foliage is continuous in early to mid-summer, but care must be taken in late summer not to remove flower buds for the next spring.

STANDARD OR TREE AZALEAS AND ESPALIERS

Any azalea that grows rapidly with a straight stem can be trained to a standard or tree form. The Southern Indians and some Glenn Dale varieties work well as standards. In cooler areas, the Kaempferis might also be used.

Single stem plants grown from cuttings are preferred, with no pinching until the desired height of the standard is obtained. Pinching of the top results in branching followed by additional pinching until a compact head is formed. The leaves and young shoots developing on the stem or trunk should be rubbed off as they occur. Rubbing off keeps the stem smooth and clear of any stubble rather than allowing the shoots to develop and then later having to cut them off.

Special standards of the Belgian and Rutherford hybrids are grafted on a single stem of other azalea plants. The green grafting technique is briefly described in the chapter on propagation and is usually done in the deep South or on the west coast in greenhouses or shade structures.

Open, loose growing azaleas are ideal for espalier work because they can be developed into a form or special design. Constant pruning is required to maintain the desired decorative effect on a wall or trellis.

The standard and espalier azaleas are generally grown as container plants and require the same maintenance previously described as well as skillful pruning.

This standard azalea makes a handsome container plant, however, it is also quite effective in the landscape.

The branching habit, trunk, and shallow and often gnarled root system of azaleas are especially attractive features of the bonsai.

The formal design of this standard has a dramatic effect in the home or on the patio.

Companion Plants
for the
Azalea Garden

The flower colors, foliage texture, and habit of growth of the plants in this garden blend well with azaleas.

Companion plants selected for the azalea garden should be adaptable to acid soils and generally shade tolerant. The plant collector or hobbiest selects plants to grow in his garden, while others select plants as the basic material to develop a garden.

Azalea foliage is considered as a fine to medium texture. The companion plants should be selected for their foliage texture, habit of growth, and other characteristics, such as flowers, that will blend and enhance the azaleas and your garden design.

Plants such as dogwoods, redbuds, fothergilla, crabapples, and others may be selected to add to the floral season. Other plants might add color before or after the azaleas have finished blooming, such as mountain laurel, stewartia, camellias along with numerous bulbs and herbaceous plants.

Fragrance can be added to the azalea garden with the addition of such plants as styrax, osmanthus or tea olive, daphne, and others.

There are many excellent berried plants like hollies and viburnums for the fall and winter, and in the spring, the blue fruit of mahonia.

The plants can be selected for their foliage alone, whether it is evergreen or deciduous. Some of the handsome evergreen shrubs frequently used with azaleas include aucuba, boxwoods, conifers, hollies, osmanthus, mahonia, danae, euonymus, and cherry laurels. Many deciduous plants such as sourwood, euonymus, fothergilla, and others, add color with their fall foliage. Perennial plants can vary from the large deciduous foliage of a hosta to the evergreen grasslike foliage of liriope, or the evergreen foliage of pachysandra. Both heuchera or coral bells and strawberry begonia or saxafraga are excellent perennials with attractive foliage and flowers. Equally important are the numerous wildflowers and ferns indigenous to each area.

A garden could be designed using only plants of the Heath family, including the sourwood tree with its attractive late spring flowers and excellent fall foliage. The beautiful evergreen plants are rhododendrons and mountain laurel or *Kalmia;* the evergreen or deciduous species of *Leucothoe;* the numerous vacciniums, or blue berries, heaths and heathers, *Leiophyllum, Elliottia, Menziesia, Enkianthus,* and trailing arbutus.

Many Southern azalea gardens may include only five basic plants, azaleas, camellias, hollies, liriope, and dogwoods.

Select plants hardy to your climatic zone. Since most azalea gardens are shaded with tall trees overhead the companion plants should also be shade tolerant and adapted to the same acid soils. The comprehensive list included will serve as a guide in selecting the companion plants. This list cannot be complete for each climatic zone, but hopefully it will serve as a general guide to the diversity of plant materials available. Select the plants carefully on their own qualities and the role they are to fill in the garden.

The gardener's challenge is not to find suitable companion plants for the azalea garden, but to select them with discrimination and restraint.

SMALL TO MEDIUM-SIZE TREES

Name	Zone*	Type**	Remarks
Acer palmatum Japanese maple	6 to 8b	D	Small rounded trees, palmately lobed leaves. Some finely divided, numerous cultivars.
Amelanchier laevis Serviceberry or Shadbush	4 to 9	D	White flowers in early spring, yellow to red fall foliage. Other species available.
Cercis canadensis Red bud	4 to 9	D	Attractive lavender-pink flowers in early spring. White flowered cultivar available.
Chionanthus virginicus Fringe tree	4 to 9	D	Lacy white flowers, native, C. retusa, Oriental fringe tree, good, Zones 6 to 9.
Cornus florida Flowering dogwood	4 to 9	D	Favorite native small tree, noted for its white bracts. Many new cultivars, Springtime, Cloud 9, Cherokee Princess. Dwarf flowered forms and weeping trees also available.
Cornus florida Cherokee Chief dogwood	5 to 8b	D	Deep rosy bracts, Jr. Miss, best in the deep South.

*Hardiness Zone.
**E represents evergreen; D represents deciduous.

Iris cristata, *Crested Iris*

Asarum shuttleworthi, *Mottled Wildginger*

Aucuba japonica, *Japanese Aucuba*

Shortia galacifolia, *Oconeebells*

Viburnum plicatum tomentosum, *Doublefile Viburnum*

Chionathus virginicus, *Fringe Tree*

Cyclamen neopolitan, *Cyclamen*

Zephyranthes atamosco,
Rain Lily

Viola pedata, *Birdfoot Violet*

Trillium grandiflorum, *Snow Trillium*

Name	Zone*	Type**	Remarks
Cornus kousa 　　Chinese dogwood	6 to 8	D	Interesting white pointed bracts. Flowers later than C. Florida. Good fall foliage.
Eribotrya japonica 　　Loquat	8a to 10	E	Large leathery foliage. Fragrant flowers.
Franklinia alatamaha 　　Franklinia	6 to 8	D	Large single white flowers in late summer. Excellent fall foliage.
Gordonia lasianthus 　　Gordonia	8b to 10	D	Used in warmer areas of Zone 9.
Halesia carolina 　　Silver bell	5 to 9	D	Early bell shape white flowers, native.
Ilex opaca 　　American holly	6 to 9	E	Tall pyramidal, singular to entire leaves; red to yellow fruit. Selected cultivars. Native.
Ilex rotunda	8b to 10	E	Pyramidal tree; entire leaves; red fruit.
Magnolia virginiana 　　Sweetbay magnolia	6 to 10	Semi-E	Leaves whitish beneath, white fragrant flowers. Native.
Oxydendrum arboreum 　　Sourwood	5 to 9	D	Cluster of white flowers in late spring; brilliant scarlet fall foliage. Native.
Pinus strobus 　　White pine	5 to 8b	E	Blue-green needles. Holds branches. Numerous other species available for various areas. Native.
Prunus caroliniana 　　Cherrylaurel	8 to 10	E	Round head. Creamy white flowers. Withstands shearing. Native.
Prunus species 　　Flowering cherry	5 to 8	D	Various species and cultivars. Best in sun or light shade.
Pyrus calleryana 　　Bradford pear	5 to 8	D	White flowers in early spring. Bronze red fall foliage.

*Hardiness Zone.
**E represents evergreen; D represents deciduous.

Name	Zone*	Type**	Remarks
Taxodium distichum Baldcypress	6 to 10	D	Deciduous conifer; does well in moist areas. Native.
Tsuga canadensis Canada hemlock	4 to 9a	E	Excellent evergreen; withstands shearing; numerous cultivar forms. Native.
Rhus glabra Smooth sumac	6 to 9	D	Compound leaves, red fruit head. Orange red fall foliage. Similar to Staghorn Sumac.
Rhus copallina Shiny sumac	7 to 9	D	Compound leaves, irregular small tree. Glossy, red fall foliage. Native.
Stewartia pseudo-camellia Japanese stewartia	6 to 8b	D	Small tree, white flowers in late spring. Attractive fall foliage.
Styrax japonica Japanese snowbell	6 to 9a	D	White bell shape blooms. Styrax obassia rare. Very handsome in flower.

SHRUBS

Name	Zone*	Type**	Size	Remarks
Abelia grandiflora Glossy abelia	7 to 10	E	6 to 8'	Pink flowers in summer. Glossy foliage. Sherwood—dwarf form.
Aucuba japonica Japanese aucuba	7 to 10	E	4 to 6'	Glossy foliage, variegated types. Sexes separate. Large red fruit in winter.
Camellia japonica Camellia	7b to 10	E	8 to 20'	Numerous cultivars; select adaptable cultivars. Other species C. sasanqua. Fall flowering.
Cephalotaxus harringtonia Japanese plum-yew	7 to 10	E	10 to 20'	Attractive needle foliage; spreading type available.
Cleyera japonica Cleyera	7b to 9	E	6 to 12'	Glossy foliage; white flowers.

*Hardiness Zone.
**E represents evergreen; D represents deciduous.

Name	Zone*	Type**	Size	Remarks
Corylopsis sinensis Chinese witchhazel	6 to 8B	D	10 to 15′	Yellow flowers in early spring.
Danae racemosa Alexandrian-laurel	7 to 10	E	3 to 5′	Attractive glossy foliage, red fruit. Spreading habit.
Euonymus alatus compacta Dwarf winged euonymus	5 to 8b	D	6 to 8′	Fall foliage, vivid scarlet.
Euonymus japonicus Microphyllus, Japanese euonymus	7b to 9b	E	1 to 2′	Similar to boxwood, subject to scale insect.
Fothergilla gardeni Dwarf fothergilla	6 to 8b	D	3 to 4′	Native, white terminal flowers. Excellent orange to scarlet fall foliage. Two large species available.
Gardenia jasminoides Gardenia	8 to 9	E	6 to 8′	White fragrant flowers. G. radicans, dwarf species 3 to 4′.
Hamamelis mollis Chinese witchhazel	6 to 8b	D	8 to 20′	Fragrant yellow flowers in late winter.
Hydrangea quercifolia Oakleaf hydrangea	6 to 9	D	5 to 8′	Native. White flowers late spring. Reddish fall foliage. H. macrophylla—blue flowers in summer.
Ilex cornuta Burford holly	7 to 10	E	10 to 20′	Glossy foliage, red fruit. Dwarf Burford smaller; Rotunda dwarf, spiny foliage; Carissa, dwarf, terminal spine.
Ilex crenata Helleri Japanese holly	7 to 9	E	3 to 5′	Dwarf, small foliage. Numerous cultivars available.
Ilex decidua Possumhaw holly	6 to 9	D	10 to 20′	Native, red fruit in clusters.

*Hardiness Zone.
**E represents evergreen; D represents deciduous.

Name	Zone*	Type**	Size	Remarks
Ilex vomitoria Yaupon holly	7 to 10	E	10 to 25'	Native, red fruit, can be sheared. Nana—dwarf, but no fruit.
Kalmia latifolia Mountain laurel	5 to 8b	E	8 to 20'	White to pink flowers late spring. Handsome native.
Leucothoe axillaris Coast leucothoe	7 to 9	E	4 to 6'	Native, excellent foliage; L. fontanesiana, larger, Zone 6 to 8; L. populifolia, Zone 7 to 9.
Mahonia pinnata Cluster mahonia	7 to 9a	E	6 to 10'	Compound leaves, yellow flowers, blue fruit. Mahonia beali, coarser foliage, zone 7 to 9a.
Myrica cerifera Wax-myrtle	8 to 10	E	12 to 20'	Fragrant foliage. Gray fruit on female plants. Native.
Nandina domestica Nandina	7 to 10	E	6 to 8'	Compound leaves, white flowers, red fruit in clusters.
Osmanthus fragrans Sweet osmanthus	8 to 10	E	12 to 20'	Fragrant small flowers. Osmanthus x fortunei, holly-like foliage, fragrant flowers. O. heterophylus, hardy to Zone 7.
Pieris japonica Japanese pieris	6 to 9	E	6 to 10'	Drooping white flowers in clusters, early spring, lustrous foliage.
Pittosporum tobira Japanese pittosporum	9 to 10	E	8 to 10'	Attractive foliage, fragrant creamy white flowers in late spring.
Prunus laurocerasus Otto luykin laurel	7 to 9	E	3 to 5'	Lustrous leaves 3 to 5" long; spreading shrubs. Zabeliana—larger.
Taxus x media Brownii yew	5 to 7	E	8 to 10'	Dense, rounded form. Numerous cultivars available.

*Hardiness Zone.
**E represents evergreen; D represents deciduous.

Name	Zone*	Type**	Size	Remarks
Vaccinium ashei Rabbiteye blueberry	7b to 9	D	8 to 15'	Native, fruit edible; V. arboreum semi-evergreen. Difficult to transplant.
Viburnum x juddi Judd viburnum	6 to 8	D	6 to 8'	Fragrant clustered white flowers; early spring. Viburnam x burkwoodi, semi-evergreen.
Viburnum plicatum Japanese viburnum	5 to 8	D	8 to 10'	Snowball flowers. Mariesii and Lomarth—new cultivars.
Viburnum odoratissimum Sweet viburnum	9 to 10	E	10 to 12'	Glossy foliage, clusters of fragrant white flowers.

PERENNIALS AND GROUND COVERS

Name	Zone*	Height	Blooming Season	Remarks
Ajuga reptans Carpet bugle	3 to 9	6 to 9"	Spring	Blue flowers, spreads rapidly. Various cultivars available.
Aquilegia canadensis Columbine	4 to 9	12 to 24"	Spring	Scarlet and yellow flowers. Naturalizes garden. Hybrids available. Native.
Asarum canadense Wildginger	3 to 8b	6"	–	Deciduous, spreading, flowers inconspicuous.
Asarum shuttleworthi Mottled wildginger	6 to 9	4 to 6"	–	Mottled evergreen leaves, spreads slowly. May be called Hexastylis. Native.
Aspidistra elatior Castiron plant	8b to 10	12 to 18"	–	Tough evergreen foliage plant for deep South. Withstands heavy shade.
Astilbe x arendsii Hybrid astilbe	6 to 8b	24"	Late spring	Fluffy spikes of flowers, white, pink to purple, compound leaves.

*Hardiness Zone.
**E represents evergreen; D represents deciduous.

Name	Zone*	Height	Blooming Season	Remarks
Dicentra spectabilis Bleeding heart	4 to 8b	12 to 24"	Spring	Pink heart-shaped flowers.
Epigaea repens Trailing arbutus	3 to 8b	4 to 6"	Early spring	Trailing evergreen, fragrant white to pink flowers, difficult to transplant. Native.
Epimedium grandiflorum Epimedium	4 to 8b	6 to 9"	Early spring	Partial evergreen, spreading, white flowers. Various colors available.
Euonymus fortunei Wintergreen	5 to 10	6 to 18"	—	Evergreen ground cover, several cultivars available.
Ferns	—	—	—	Numerous species available for all areas, excellent evergreen forms available.
Galax aphylla Galax	4 to 8b	6 to 12"	Spring	Evergreen leaves, spike of white flowers. Native.
Hedera helix English ivy	5 to 10	—	—	Evergreen vines, numerous cultivars available.
Helleborus orientalis Lenten rose	6 to 9	12 to 18"	Early spring	Evergreen, nodding flowers, white to purple, basal leaves.
Heuchera sanquinea Coral bells	4 to 9	12 to 24"	Spring	Basal rounded leaves, spike of bell-like flowers, white to red.
Hosta species Hosta or Plantain lily	4 to 9	12 to 24"	Late summer	Numerous species, excellent foliage, from small to large. White to lavender flowers.
Iberis sempervirens Candytuft	4 to 9	8 to 12"	Spring	Evergreen low plant; white flowers; many cultivars.
Iris crestata Crested iris	4 to 9	6 to 24"	Spring	Low spreading native plant. Blue flowers, shade tolerant.

*Hardiness Zone.

Name	Zone*	Height	Blooming Season	Remarks
Iris tectorum Root iris	7 to 9	12 to 18″	Spring	Blue flowers, evergreen creeping foliage; Louisiana iris, shade tolerant.
Mertensia virginica Virginia bluebells	4 to 8a	18 to 24″	Spring	Attractive pink fading to blue flowers. Native.
Phlox divaricata Blue phlox	4 to 9	8 to 12″	Spring	Spreading plants, blue flowers. Native.
Phlox stolonifera Creeping phlox	4 to 9	6 to 12″	Spring	Low creeping plant. Violet to purple flowers.
Polygonatum biflorum Solomon's seal	4 to 9	24 to 36″	Spring	Attractive bell shape yellowish-white nodding flowers. Native.
Primula auricula Primrose	4 to 8a	8″	Spring	Colorful flowers. Best in cool areas. Numerous species available.
Rohdea japonica Nippon-lily	8b to 10	12 to 15″	—	Leathery, long foliage. Also used as house plant.
Sanguinaria canadensis Bloodroot	4 to 9a	4 to 6″	Early spring	Attractive white flowers in early spring. Native.
Saxifragra stolifera Strawberry geranium	7 to 9	6 to 12″	Spring	White veined evergreen leaves; low spreading; attractive small white flowers.
Sedum ternatum Stonecrop	5 to 9	6″	Spring	Low spreading bluish white flowers; other species available.
Shortia galacifolia Oconee-bells	4 to 8b	6″	Early spring	Attractive evergreen foliage; bell-like white flowers in early spring. Native.
Smilacina racemosa False Solomon's seal	4 to 9	24 to 30″	Spring	Small white flowers in terminal clusters. Native.

*Hardiness Zone.

Name	Zone*	Height	Blooming Season	Remarks
Tiarella cordifolia Foam flower	4 to 9	6 to 12″	Spring	Spreading native plant. Attractive spike of small white flowers.
Vinca minor Periwinkle	5 to 9	4 to 6″	Spring	Evergreen ground cover. White or blue flowers.
Violia species Violets	4 to 9	6 to 8″	Spring	Numerous species. White to blue flowers.

BULBS

Name	Zone*	Height	Blooming Season	Remarks
Allium sp. Flowering onion	4 to 10	12 to 36″	Spring	Attractive small flowers in round clusters. Grass-like foliage.
Anemone blanda Blue anemone	6 to 9	6 to 8″	Spring	Tuberous roots, attractive blue flowers.
Chiondora luciliae Glory-of-the-snow	7 to 9	24″	Spring	Small bell shape flowers in clusters.
Colchicum sp. Autumn crocus	4 to 9	4 to 6″	Fall	Several species, pink to lavender blue flowers.
Convalaria majalis Lily-of-the-valley	4 to 8	6 to 8″	Spring	Fragrant white bell shape flowers.
Crinum sp. Crinum	8 to 10	18 to 24″	Summer	Large lily-like white to red flowers in summer; some species evergreen.
Crocus sp. Crocus	5 to 9	3 to 6″	Early	Numerous species and varieties; white, yellow, blue/lavender flowers.
Cyclamen neapolitanum Neapolitan cyclamen	6 to 8b	3 to 6″	Late summer	Attractive white to pink flowers; attractive mottled leaves from fall to spring.

*Hardiness Zone.

Name	Zone*	Height	Blooming Season	Remarks
Galanthus nivalis Snowdrops	4 to 9	12″	Spring	Attractive white flowers.
Hyacinthus orientalis Hyacinth	6 to 10	12 to 15″	Spring	Fragrant white, pink to purple flowers.
Liriope muscari Lilyturf	6 to 10	12 to 18″	Late summer	Evergreen coarse grass-like foliage. White to blue flowers. L. spicata, spreading.
Lycoris sp. Spider lily	6 to 9	12 to 18″	Late	L. aurea, deep South, yellow flowers. L. radiata, red, and L. squamigera, pink.
Narcissus sp. Daffodil	5 to 10	12 to 18″	Spring	Popular garden bulb, naturalizes.
Scilla sibirica Siberian squill	4 to 10	6″	Early	Attractive blue flowers. Spring Beauty, good deep blue.
Trillium sp. Trillium	6 to 9	12 to 18″	Spring	Several species. Attractive, native wild flower.
Tulipa sp. Tulip	4 to 8a	12 to 18″	Spring	Attractive flowering bulb. Use pre-cooled bulbs for deep South.
Zephyranthes atamosco Rain lily	8 to 10	12 to 24″	Spring	Upright white solitary lily flowers. Native.
Zephyranthes candida Autumn rain lily	8 to 10	12″	Late summer	White flowers, late summer, early fall.

*Hardiness Zone.

Propagation

Azaleas generally are easy to propagate, however, not all species or varieties may be propagated by the same method. A gardener can choose one or more methods, each having advantages and disadvantages, and each requiring specific timing and procedure. Fundamentally, azaleas can be propagated by seed, stem cutting, layering, grafting, and by division.

Propagation by seed is the most desirable method for many of the deciduous azaleas and for those varieties which are difficult to propagate from cutting or other means. Plants propagated by seeds, however, will be variable, flower colors varying from plant to plant. This, of course, is an advantage for the hybridizer or gardener seeking new plants. It is not uncommon to propagate the evergreen azaleas from seed, but again, one must expect a great deal of variability from seedlings since most of the evergreen azaleas that we commonly grow as garden plants are hybrids and are extremely variable. Seeds of the common Snow Kurume azalea might offer a range of colorful plants from lavenders to reds, pinks, and whites. The native azaleas are generally very difficult to propagate from stem cuttings, and for this reason are propagated from seed or by layering.

Seed capsules are normally collected in late fall as the pods begin to turn brown, but before the pods completely crack open. The season varies from September through November, depending on individual plants. The seed capsules can be stored during the winter months and allowed to dry until they open, at which time the seed can be separated from the capsule. Rhododendron or azalea seed are very small, and one seed capsule will offer a large quantity of seed — up to 500 or more. The seed can be germinated immediately or stored until spring. However, azalea seed can be germinated during the winter months in a greenhouse or in the home.

This is a 3 year-old Kurume azalea seedling.

Compare the sizes of the 3 month-old rooted cutting, the 6 month-old rooted cutting, and the 2 to 9 month-old seedlings of R. kiusianum.

42

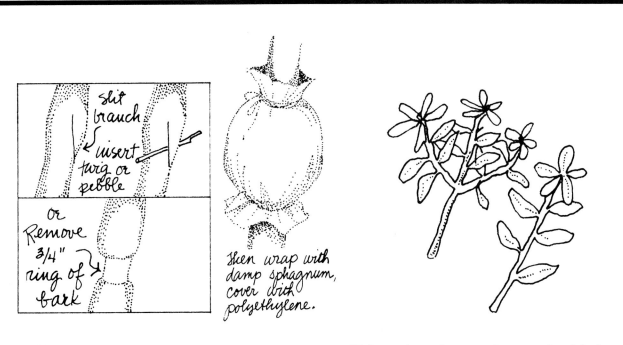

Air layering gives you a choice of more branches to root than soil layering does. Be sure the sphagnum is not soggy and that the plastic is well sealed to prevent loss of moisture.

Take cuttings when new shoots are 2 to 3 inches long. Strip off lower leaves that may touch the rooting medium.

Sterilized plastic boxes such as shoe boxes or freezer boxes are ideal for seed propagation units. The plastic box can be sterilized with alcohol or by using a bleach solution of 1 to 20, washing the inside of the box. Next, a rooting medium is needed, preferably shredded sphagnum moss. The sphagnum moss should be soaked until throughly wet, and then squeezed dry. Two inches of moss is spread over the bottom of the box, and the fine seeds are scattered over the medium and lightly watered in. The box is covered and stored at a temperature of 65° to 75°F. in an area of indirect light. Germination normally will start within two to four weeks. Remove the cover after the seeds have germinated. The small seedlings can be kept indefinitely in sphagnum as a "storage unit" without fertilizer for several years. Sphagnum moss is an ideal sterile medium and reduces the problem of damping off a common fungus disease.

The seedlings are ready for transplanting into other flats or small pots after several true leaves have appeared. Small wooden tweezers can be made that reduce damaging the small plants during transplanting. The potting medium should consist of equal parts of sand and peat moss or leaf mold. To grow on, plant the seedlings in nursery beds or cold frames in the spring. Keep the young plants in active growth with light applications of fertilizer and water, but harden off, or withhold fertilizer and water four to six weeks before frost. Avoid using hard water because it will raise the pH. Rainwater, distilled or de-ironized water should be used in regions of hard water.

Deciduous azaleas, started from seed, normally will flower in three to five years. Seedlings of evergreen azaleas will flower earlier, usually in two to three years. As the plants develop, pinch the terminal growth in order to develop shapely, multibranched plants. To produce seedlings rapidly, grow them under additional light. Florescent light units offer a good opportunity to experiment with the addition of light in the growth of azaleas and other plants. Twelve to sixteen hours of light are generally recommended. Evergreen azaleas can be kept growing continuously in a greenhouse with additional lights for as long as two years without a rest period.

Propagation by cuttings is generally practiced with the evergreen azaleas. While it is basically true that the cutting-grown plants will develop like the parent plant, sports or mutations do occur with variable plants such as the azaleas, and the cutting-grown progeny may be different from the parent source. Cuttings are made from new wood, normally in the months of June and July. The new growth should break with a snap when they are ready. Cuttings should be 3 to 4 inches long with all leaves removed from ⅓ to ½ of the basal area. Rooting hormones on the cuttings will aid in reducing the time required for rooting, and for varieties which are difficult to root, the rooting percentage is improved. Rooting hormones mixed with a fungicide such as ferbam (Fermate) or benomyl (Benlate) are used by commercial growers. Quick dip liquid hormones are used when a fungicide is applied on the rooting medium.

Cuttings can be rooted in a greenhouse where the humidity is high, or outdoors in a mist unit, or in shade covered flats or boxes outdoors. For small quantities of cuttings, use a plastic box, or enclose a flat in plastic like a tent. The rooting medium depends on individual preference and method of rooting. The two common media are equal parts of sand and peat, or peat and perlite. Sand mixtures are preferred if propagating under mist. Clean sand should be used, and the rooting medium should be used for only one batch of cuttings.

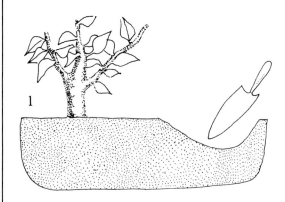

Select a vigorous, young branch growing close to the ground or one flexible enough to bend. Mark a point approximately 12 inches from the end of the branch just below a node. Make a 4" deep hole directly beneath this point. Mix soil with equal parts of peat moss and sand.

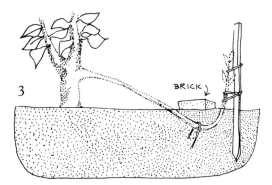

Place a brick or stone on the soil directly above the layered stem section; this will keep the soil firm and will help retain moisture. In cold winter areas, spread a mulch of leaves over the layer to protect it, leaving the tip and several of the leaves exposed.

Cuttings should be stuck to about ½ of their length, lightly watered, and enclosed in the plastic units. The propagation units should be kept out of direct sunlight, unless a mist unit is used. Small mist units are available commercially, or you can make your own by using mist nozzles on 3-foot centers at 18 to 24 inches above the bed. The mist units should be in a wind-free area, such as a greenhouse, or if used

44

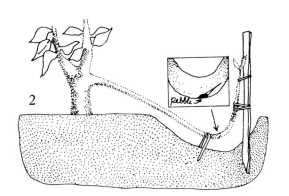

At the marked point on the underside of the branch, make a slanting cut half way through; wedge in a small twig or pebble. Bend branch into the hole; anchor it to the soil with a heavy wire loop. Bring the end of the branch to a vertical position and stake. Fill hole with the prepared soil; firm; then water thoroughly.

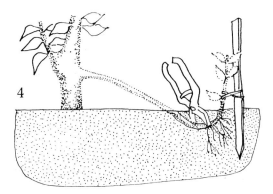

Check to see if the layer has rooted by carefully removing the soil on top of the layer. When the roots are well established, sever the stem from the parent plant just below the original cut.

in the open, the sides should be enclosed, and they should be in a light shade area.

Azalea cuttings will normally root in four to six weeks, and will then be ready for transplanting into potting soil high in organic matter. Light applications of fertilizer to the rooted cuttings during the growing season will speed up their growth.

Deciduous cultivars of the Ghent, Mollis, and Knaphill hybrids can be rooted by cuttings. The deciduous native azaleas, however, can be very difficult to propagate by cuttings. There is extreme variability among cultivars and the stoloniferous species such as *R. nudiflorium*, Pinxterbloom azalea root easier than the non-stoloniferous types. There are two problems in rooting deciduous azaleas: First is rooting the cutting, and secondly, inducing new growth following rooting. Deciduous cuttings failing to develop vegetative growth following rooting have a very low survival over the first winter.

A modified method of stem cuttings is layering. Although it is a slow method, it is reliable if only a few plants, particularly the deciduous types are to be propagated. A branch of the mother plant is pegged down into the soil. Layering can be done at any season, but late spring or summer is preferred. Select a one- or two-year-old low hanging branch to bury. The stem can be wounded by scraping the bark or making a cut 1 to 1½ inches long. Bury the branch 3 inches deep at the point of the cutting and twist the top of the branch upward. Peg the branch down with wire, or with a brick or stone placed on top. Cover the wounded branch with peat moss or humus and keep moist throughout the growing season. Layering is slow, and often a year or more is required before the new plant can be removed on its own roots.

Air layering is a modification of the soil layers and is used on deciduous azaleas and rhododendrons. Air layers are usually made in late spring on last year's wood. Make an upward cut of 1 inch or longer on the stem. Dust the cut surface with hormone powder, and add sphagnum moss between the cut. Pack the wound area with a handful of moist sphagnum, and seal the wound with plastic and tie it tightly at both ends. A plastic bag with the bottom cut off is frequently used for the airtight wrap. It is often advisable to cover the plastic wrap with aluminum foil to reduce the temperature and prevent drying out. Air layers made in the spring usually are sufficiently rooted by fall and can then be removed. Keep the new plant in a protected location over the winter. If the layer is not rooted in the fall, it should remain on the branch until the second year.

Native azaleas can also be propagated by root cuttings. This technique was modified after observing young plants developing from roots left after digging plants in the wild. Native plants can also be root pruned. The severed roots will often form a new vegetative shoot which can be removed one or two years later. Root cuttings, 3 inches in length and pencil size in diameter, can be propagated at all seasons of the year. The most favorable time, however, is early spring. The root pieces are layed horizontally in a box of peat moss or sphagnum moss and covered with the same. The root pieces develop new roots and a vegetative shoot within the growing season.

Grafting is not a common method for propagating azaleas, but it is used for growing an unusual plant which may be difficult to root from cuttings, or to produce unusual plant forms such as the tree azaleas. Grafting has also been used on the Ghent and Knaphill azaleas and with evergreen rhododendrons.

The root stock or understock for grafting should be in an active state of growth, while the top wood or scion should be in a dormant condition. This may present some difficulties and the gardener may have to resort to greenhouse facilities for starting the understock.

A modified side graft or a wedge graft is generally used. Match the cambium layers of the scion and understock before securing the graft union with a rubber band. To keep the graft union from drying out, wrap it with damp sphagnum moss and cover it with plastic as in

an air layer. If the graft union is at ground level, the plant can be buried or mounded to cover the union.

Green grafting is usually done outdoors for tree azaleas when both the scion and understock are in an active state of growth and after the new growth is nearly hardened off. Use a wedge graft and match the cambium layers before wrapping the graft union with damp sphagnum moss. Cover the entire graft union and scion with a plastic bag. Keep the graft from direct sunlight or protect it by covering with a paper bag. The graft should be healed in a month and the new scion showing active growth. When this is observed, open the plastic bag gradually by punching a few holes. Slowly, over a period of several weeks, increase the air by opening more holes in the plastic bag, until it can be completely removed. The young grafted plant should be handled as carefully as rooted cuttings the first season.

The stoloniferous species of native azaleas can be multiplied by dividing. The plant should be divided during the dormant season which is from the late fall until early spring. It is advisable to cut back the top growth of the plant after dividing the root system. The new plants propagated by division should produce flower buds within two or three seasons.

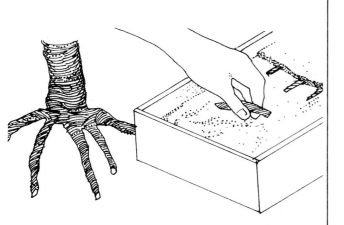

Root cuttings should be 3 inches in length and pencil size in diameter. The root pieces should be layered horizontally in a box of peat moss or sphagnum moss and then covered with the same.

These propagation units are excellent for seed propagation.

Diseases and Insect Pests

Fortunately azaleas are relatively free of diseases and insect pests. The chart lists the common pests that may be observed.

Do not confuse poor cultural conditions or winter injury with injuries from diseases or insects.

Azalea petal blight is serious in the warmer southern areas, and is more noticeable in the mid- to late season varieties. Native azaleas and the Kurume azalea, while not resistant to the disease, are seldom troubled with the problem. Hopefully, as new fungicides become available, better controls will be available.

Lace wing or lace bug is the common insect of evergreen azaleas, and is generally observed after the early Kurume azaleas have finished flowering.

Use the following precautions with pesticides:
1. Read the label and follow all precautions.
2. Handle pesticides with care and respect. Improperly used, they can be injurious to man, animals, and plants.
3. Store pesticides in locked cabinets away from children and foods.
4. Use rubber gloves when mixing sprays. Work on windward side of area. Avoid drifts or inhaling pesticides.
5. Avoid contact of pesticides with nose, eyes, and mouth.
6. Wash immediately after using pesticides. Do not eat, drink, or smoke after using pesticides until you have washed.
7. Wear protective clothing if at all possible. Change clothing if contaminated with pesticides.
8. Do not use herbicides (weedkillers) in the same sprayer used for pesticides. Have different sprayers and mark them accordingly.
9. Do not mix pesticides unless you are

Leaf gall results in malformed, enlarged, thick fleshy leaves that are pale green changing to velvety grayish white.

This damage is a result of lace wing or lace bug.

48

These worms are datura larvae which feed on native azaleas.

sure they are compatible.

10. Dispose of empty containers by placing in plastic bag before placing in trash or taking to disposal centers.
11. Use only recommended pesticides. Contact your local County Agent for specific recommendations.
12. Follow directions and do not overdose.

Pesticides properly used are an important tool for good gardening.

DISEASES AND INSECT PESTS

Diseases	Control Measures	Diseases	Control Measures
Leaf Gall: malformed, enlarged, thick, fleshy leaves, pale green changing to velvety grayish white.	A problem in wet seasons. Hand pick galls and destroy. Spray early at first sign of trouble with Captan or Zineb.	Botrytis Petal Blight: gray mold on petals, black spores visible with hand lens.	Problem in midseason. Spray with Thylate or Zineb two or three times per week.
		Leaf Spot: brownish spots first on underside causes leaves to drop.	Spray with Captan or Zineb weekly.
Petal Blight: water spot petals, progressing to collapsed brownish, shiny flowers.	Soil drench before flowering with terrachlor or Turban. Serous on large flowered and mid- to late season plants. Spray flowers three times per week with Thylate, Thiram or Zineb.	Phytophthora Blight: brown and silver spotted leaves, more common on rhododendrons.	Remove diseased leaves. Spray with fermate or Parzate
		Rhododendron Wilt: wilting of stems, entire plant dying back; stem when cut shows brown streaks.	Soil borne and serious with rhododendrons in poorly drained spots. Use soil drench Dexon, Truban, two to three times per season.

Insects	Control Measures	Insects	Control Measures
Lace Wing: small insect with lace-like wing; leaves grayish green, brown to black spots on underside where nymphs hatched.	Malathion, zectram at 7 to 10 day intervals. Systemic disytox application after early flowering.	Red Spider Mites: feeding on underside of leaves; mites visible with hand lens; leaves appear stippled off-color and turning brown.	Malathion, diazinon, Kelthane at 7 day intervals on underside of leaves.
Leaf Miner: small caterpillar mining inside leaf; comes out folding back edge of leaf to pupate.	Generally not serious. Malathion, diazinon— 7 to 10 day intervals.	Datura Larvae: large gregarious blueish black caterpillar feeding on native azaleas and blueberries.	Malathion, diazinon.
Scale: small white cottony scales in leaf axils and on twigs.	Malathion, diazinon at 7 to 10 day intervals.	Nematodes: dieback or general decline; leaves off-color or stunted; root system matted or restricted by feeding of nematodes.	Nematocide.
Mealy Bugs: powdery gray, mottled insects ⅛ inch in size, on leaf axils and flower buds.	Same control as for Scale.	Rabbits: feeding on young leaves and stems; very fond of gumpo azaleas.	Thiram spray, animal sprays, or climatic source.

Azalea or Rhododendron

The classification of plants is often confusing to the gardener and is a subject which evokes deep discussion and occasional modifications.

Plants are classified botanically by division, and these in turn by classes, orders, families, genera, and species.

Azaleas would thus be classified as follows:
Division—Spermatophyta—seed bearing.
Class—Dicotyledoneae—two cotyledons in the embryo as contrasted to one in Monocotyledons, such as the grasses.
Order—Ericales, related plants.
Family—Ericaceae—Heath family.
Genus—Rhododendron
Subgenus—Anthodendron

Thus, the azaleas, botanically speaking, are Rhododendrons, but historically, this was not always the case. Linnaeus, often referred to as the father of plant taxonomy, established the genus Rhododendron in 1753, and azaleas were placed in a separate genus based on the deciduous species of azalea he had at hand. Following the discovery of evergreen azaleas, the genus Azalea was dropped and these plants were included in a series, or group, within the genus Rhododendron.

So the classification stands today, but the question of azalea or rhododendron is still unsettled. The gardener and the horticulturist, while recognizing that botanically azaleas are Rhododendrons, will continue to use the common name, azalea, for the deciduous and small-leaved types, and the name rhododendron for the large evergreen species and varieties. This can be somewhat justified since there are both azaleas and rhododendrons with the same cultivar names, for example Appleblossom and Pink Pearl azalea, as well as Appleblossom and Pink Pearl rhododendron.

The Heath (Ericaceae) family to which the rhododendrons and azaleas belong, includes more than 70 genera of plants. In this family are many plants familiar to Southern gardeners such as: mountain laurel *(Kalmia)*, sourwood *(Oxydendrum arboreum)*, sand myrtle *(Leiophyllum)*, trailing arbutus *(Epigaea repens)*, Pieris, blueberries *(Vaccinium)*, *Menziesia, Befaria, Elliottia*, heaths, heathers, and many others.

The genus Rhododendron, widely distributed throughout the world, is composed of nearly a thousand species. A genus of this size and distribution requires additional organization. Thus, two subgeneric classifications are currently in use: the Rehder system and the Hutchison system. Most botanists, particularly plant taxonomists, prefer the Rehder system of sub-genera, sections, subsections, and species, whereas, horticulturists and amateur growers usually prefer the less complicated English system proposed by Hutchison.

Under the Hutchison system, the series Azalea is subdivided into six subseries or sections. Confusion often arises in differentiating an azalea from certain species of small-leaved rhododendron. Defining characteristics do exist. Leaves and branches of the azalea in question are covered with a pubescence of flattened hairs which is lacking on some rhododendron. And, unlike some rhododendron, azalea do not have lepidote scales on their leaves. Azalea flowers, borne from terminal buds, have 5 to 10 stamens. True evergreen rhododendron generally have 10 stamens.

The flowers and the new shoots of an azalea do not always come from the same buds. Consequently, azaleas are divided into two natural groups:
A. The subseries with both flowers and leaves arising from the terminal buds. Includes evergreen and deciduous shrubs.
 1. Subseries Obtusum. The evergreen or persistent-leaved species of China, Japan,

R. prunifolium, *Plumleaf Azalea*

Korea, and Formosa. The common introduced ones include *R. kaempferi, R. kiusianum, R. macrosepalum, R. mucronatum, R. obtusum, R. poukhanense,* and *R. serpyllifolium.*

2. Subseries Tashiroi. Includes only one rare evergreen species, *R. Tashiroi,* from the Ryukyu Islands near southern Japan.

3. Subseries Schlippenbachi. Consists of seven deciduous species from Korea, China, and Japan. The three common ones are *R. quinquefolium, R. reticulatum,* and *R. schlippenbachi.*

B. The subseries bearing only flowers from the terminal flower buds. All are deciduous shrubs.

1. Subseries Luteum. (Section Pentanthera in Rehder). The species of this series are noted for their long funnel form of flower tubes and exserted stamens, as noted by our native azaleas. Fourteen native species are found in the eastern United States and one, *R. occidentale,* in the western United States. One species, *R. Flavum* (luteum) is found in southern Europe, and two species, *R. japonicum* and *R. molle,* from Japan and China.

2. Subseries Canadense (Section Rhodora in Rehder) comprises two species; *R. canadense* and *R. vaseyi* from the eastern United States, and two species, *R. albrechti* and *R. Pentaphyllum* from Japan. The flowers have very short tubes and appear bell shape with separate petals.

3. Subseries Nipponicum includes only one rare deciduous species: *R. nipponicum* from Japan.

There are still many Asian species that have not been introduced into cultivation and, as more is learned about them, they will be placed by the taxonomists in the appropriate subseries.

AZALEA NAMES

The azaleas found in gardens today are either species or hybrids.

A species is a group of native plants that have many identical fundamental characteristics which show a common relationship and origin. Thus, the Pinxterbloom azalea is named *Rhododendron nudiflorum* (often written *R. nudiflorum*). Species within any genus usually can be recognized by combinations of abstract characteristics. However, within the genus Rhododendron, taxonomists and botanists are still debating the question of species for some of the native azaleas.

Within a species, small groups of individual plants may possess, on a geographical basis, some minor variations easily recognized and referred to as a variety. A variety of the Piedmont or Florida pinxter azalea is *R. canescens candidum* and is characterized by a heavy whitish pubescence on the underside of the leaves. Local variations, such as color of flowers and habit of growth may be further defined as forms (f.). Thus, *R. calendulaceum f. aurantium* is a deep orange-red and scarlet form. *R. obtusum f. amoenum* is a small, rich magenta flowered form.

The current trend in plant taxonomy, however, is away from such subspecific classifications in favor of a broader concept of a species. This kind of taxonomic "lumping" has a strong biological basis and tends to simplify species classification.

Azalea enthusiasts soon recognize that a species is variable. Thus the selection of an outstanding plant within a species leads to the naming of a cultivar.

The majority of azaleas, especially the evergreen types, are hybrids resulting from the cross pollination of different species, varieties, and forms, or between plants from different hybrid groups.

Seedlings from such crosses may show a great deal of variability and this variability increases as additional crosses are made. Hybrid groups are frequently given names which refer to the entire group of plants, such as Glenn Dale Hybrids, Back Acres Hybrids, Satsuki Hybrids, and others.

Plants within a hybrid group may show considerable variation, due to the parental crosses, and can be difficult to classify, except by name only. For example, the foliage of Glenn Dale Azaleas within different cultivars may vary from small to large, 2 to 3 inches in length.

Special individual plants of a hybrid group or of a species may be selected and propagated vegetatively by cuttings, layering, or grafting, and are called cultivars or, literally, a "cultivated hybrid." Azalea cultivars, because of the great variability, are of tremendous importance. Many "horticultural" or "garden varieties" are actually cultivars and are listed as follows: Coral Bells, Glacier, Formosa. We might find, also, the plant listed as Coral Bells Kurume Azalea or as Glacier Glenn Dale Azalea. As we shall soon find out, many hybrid groups are extremely variable, a result of crosses of numerous parentage.

EVERGREEN OR PERSISTENT-LEAVED AZALEAS

The evergreen azaleas are the favorite garden plants of the South, but none are native to the United States. It is from species native to eastern Asia and the offshore islands that all evergreen azaleas have been derived. The evergreen azaleas have two types of leaves: spring leaves and summer (or dimorphic) leaves. The spring leaves are thinner, longer, and short-lived, dropping off in the fall — this is not a sign of weakness, but a normal shedding. The summer leaves develop in the summer at the tip of the branches. They are smaller and more leathery than spring leaves. Generally, the summer leaves remain through the winter until the following spring and sometimes longer. The evergreen azaleas, at best, may be described as partially evergreen, depending on the climatic area.

The various groups of evergreen azaleas are of long-standing and complex origin.

Southern Indian Hybrids: The Southern Indian hybrids, Indicas, were the first evergreen group introduced to the United States. The Indian Hybrids had their origin as evergreen house plants developed in Belgium and introduced to Magnolia Gardens, near Charleston, South Carolina, in 1840 and later by the old P. J. Berckman Nursery Company (later Fruitland Nursery) of Augusta, Georgia. The early imports were found to be hardy in the South, and their fame spread through all the gardens of the southeast. (The Southern Indian Hybrids were not derived only from *R. indicum*, but from numerous species and varieties.)

Some are even forms of species, such as *R. indicum, R. simsii, R. mucronatum,* and *R. phoeniceum.* The Southern Indians are generally considered tender, and are best used in Zone 8b through Zones 9 and 10. Lawsal, George Lindley Taber, and Mme. Dominique Vervaene are hardier, but still may lose their flower buds some years. The large flowers, 2 to 3½ inches across, are either single or double and exhibit a wide range of color. The common Indicas are usually fast and open growing plants, blooming early. Others are slow growing, low, spreading, dense, and generally mid- to late blooming.

A large number of the Indian hybrid cultivars were grown in Southern nurseries. A list of some of the more important, but not all of the cultivars, is as follows:

Alba Maculata (Alba): Flowers white with faint chartreuse blotch, 3 inches across, medium, spreading, midseason.

Criterion: flowers violet red with white edges and darker blotch, low, late.

Croemina: flowers violet pink, tall, midseason.

Daphne White: flowers white.

Daphne Salmon: (see Lawsal).

Dixie Beauty: flowers violet red, mid- to late season.

Duc de Rohan: flowers orange red, spreading, midseason.

Elegans Superba (Pride of Mobile): flowers light pink, 2 inches, tall, midseason.

Fielder's White: flowers white with faint chartreuse blotch, frilled, 2¾ inches, medium, spreading, early to midseason. (Tenderer than Indica Alba.)

Fisher Pink (Dodd's Pink): flowers light pink, midseason.

Formosa: flowers violet red, 3½ inches, tall, midseason.

Pink Formosa: a pink sport of Formosa.

George Lindley Taber: flowers white flushed violet red with darker blotch, 3½ inches, medium, midseason.

Giant Ruffles: flowers rose red, large, tall.

Gulf Pride: flowers light purple, a sport of *R. mucronatum.*

Indica Alba *(R. mucronatum):* flowers white, fragrant, 3 inches, medium, midseason.

Iveryana: flowers white with red flecks to rose petals, 3 inches, low, late.

Judge Solomon: flowers pink, tall, a sport of Formosa.

Lawsal (Daphne Salmon): flowers salmon pink,.2½ inches, medium, midseason.

Mme. Dominique Vervaene: flowers orange red with white margin, red blotch, 2¼ inches, medium, midseason.

Mardi Gras: flowers white with pink stripes, sport of Pride of Mobile.

Mrs. G. G. Gerbing: flowers white, sport of George Lindley Taber.

Omurasaki: flowers violet red with red blotch, 3½ inches, medium, midseason, similar to Formosa, a clone of *R. phoeniceum.*

President Claeys (President Clay): flowers
  red, 2¼ inches, tall, midseason.
Pride of Dorking: flowers carmine red,
  medium late.
Pride of Mobile (Elegans Superba): flowers
  deep rose pink, 2½ inches, tall, midseason.
Prince of Orange: flowers orange red, 2¼
  inches, medium, midseason.
Southern Charm: pink sport of Formosa.
Supreme: flowers white with chartreuse
    throat, 2½ inches, low, late.
Triomphe de Ledeberg (Moss Point Red):
  flowers orange red, 3 inches, medium,
  spreading, late.
Watermelon Red: flowers deep color, tall,
  midseason, form of Pride of Mobile.

Belgian Indian (Bel.) and Rutherford Hybrids
(R.H.): The Belgian Indian azaleas were
developed for greenhouse forcing in the mid
1800's. This work took place mainly in
Belgium and England but also in France and
Germany. From this group came many
spectacular large flowered semidouble azaleas.
The Belgian azaleas are generally considered
tender, although not many have been tried
outdoors in the South, and are now
recommended for Zones 8b through Zone 10.
After testing these plants at Callaway Gardens,
one would recommend further trial for the
deep South. The plants are generally mid- to
late season flowering.

The Rutherford Hybrids were developed
around 1920 by Bobinks and Atkins Nursery
in New Jersey and are the American addition
to the Belgian Hybrids.

A few cultivars from these two groups that
have been tested outdoors in Zone 8b through
Zone 9 are as follows:
Alaska (R.H.): flowers white with chartreuse
  blotch, single to double, 2 inches,
  midseason, slightly tender.
Albert-Elizabeth (Bel.): flowers white with
  orange-red edging, semidouble, frilled, 3

inches, excellent greenhouse forcing
  azalea.
Albion (R.H.): flowers white, hose-in-hose,
  2 inches, late.
Dorothy Gish (R.H.): flowers orange red,
  hose-in-hose, 2½ inches, midseason.
Hexe de Saffelaere (Bel.): flowers violet red,
  hose-in-hose, 2½ inches, late.
King's White (R.): flowers white, 2½ inches.
Mme. Joseph Vervaene (Bel.): flowers
  salmon with dark blotch, double.
Mother of Pearl (R.H.): flowers pale pink,
  hose-in-hose, 2½ inches, tender.
Prof. Wolters (Bel.): flowers salmon rose,
  white edge, single.
Pink Ruffles (R.H.): flowers violet red,
  hose-in-hose, semidouble, 2 inches,
  midseason.
Paul Schaeme: flowers light orange, double.
Snowbank (Cherokee White) (R.H.): flowers
  white, 2½ inches, midseason.
Vervaenena (Bel.): flowers purple red with
  white margin, double, 3 inches,
  midseason, there are various sports —
  white, orange, and salmon reds.

Additional Belgian Hybrids: New hybrids are
still being produced, primarily in California.
These hybrids have been developed for
forcing, but some are proving hardy in the
South.
Covergirl: flowers red, hose-in-hose, 3
  inches.
Desert Rose: flowers salmon rose, light
  throat, frilled, 3½ inches.
Dogwood: flowers white, 3 inches.
Easter Parade: flowers pink with white
  marbling, hose-in-hose, 3½ inches,
  midseason.
Redwings: flowers orange red, hose-in-hose,
  3 inches, midseason.
Sun Valley: flowers white, hose-in-hose, 2
  inches, early midseason.

Kurume Hybrids: The Kurume Hybrids
originated in Kurume on the island of Kyushu

and were first introduced to California in 1915. A dozen varieties were exhibited at the Panama-Pacific Exposition and were purchased by the Domoto Bros. Nursery of Hayward, California. They later introduced others known as the Domoto introductions. E. H. Wilson, a plant explorer for the Arnold Arboretum, first saw the Kurumes in Japan in 1914 and introduced a group called the Wilson's Fifty. He also encouraged Mr. John S. Ames of N. Easton, Massachusetts, to obtain a group of the plants in 1917. In 1972, Callaway Gardens received a collection of the Ames azaleas containing some of the progeny of the original Kurumes first introduced to the East. R. K. Beattie of the U.S.D.A. also introduced Kurume azaleas in 1929.

Kurumes were derived from *R. obtusum, R. kaempferi, R. kuisianum,* and *R. sataense.* Kurumes, while often considered dwarf, vary in rate of growth and most plants will develop into dense, shapely plants 4 to 6 feet in height. The plants have been excellent for greenhouse forcing, and have a full range of colors from white to pink, scarlet, lavender, and salmon, with many additional shades and tints.

The Kurumes are hardier than the Southern Indians, and are adaptable from Zone 7 to Zone 9a.

A list and description of the older Kurumes will be given first, followed by the newer hybrids. Unfortunately, many of the older varieties and the soft, pastel color forms are difficult to find in nurseries today.

Appleblossom (Ho-o): flowers pink with white throat, 1¼ inches, tall, upright.
Amoenum: flowers rich magenta, hose-in-hose, small, dense, twiggy, old variety, hardier than most, often listed as *R. obtusum japonicum,* included as a Kurume.
Amoena Coccinea: flowers carmine rose, hose-in-hose, small, dense, twiggy.
Bridesmaid: flowers salmon, upright spreading.
Christmas Cheer (Ima-shojo): flowers brilliant red, 1¼ inches, medium.
Coral Bells (Kirin): flowers shell pink, hose-in-hose, medium.
Debutante: flowers salmon pink, lighter throat, medium.
Flame (Suetsuma): flowers orange red, 1½ inches, tall.
Hinode-giri (Hino): flowers vivid red, 1½ inches, medium, compact, very common.
Hi-no-mayo: flowers rose pink, tall, upright.
Hino Supreme: flowers dark crimson, 1½ inches, medium.
Hortensia: flowers violet red, 1½ inches, medium.
Iro-hayama (Dainty): flowers pale lavender, white margin.
Koromo-shikibu: flowers violet pink, petals separate, narrow and strap-like, distinct, medium.
Mizu-no-yamabuki: flowers creamy white, small, medium.
Mountain Laurel: flowers flesh pink, often fading to nearly white, medium.
Peach Blow: flowers peach pink, medium, upright.
Pink Pearl (Azuma-kagami): flowers salmon rose, hose-in-hose, medium to tall, upright.
Salmon Beauty: flowers salmon pink, hose-in-hose, medium.
Snow: flowers hose-in-hose, 1½ inches, old flowers persist, medium, upright.
Vesuvius: flowers salmon red, medium.
Yaeshojo: flowers orange red, hose-in-hose, tall, upright.

New Kurume hybrids have been developed on both the east and west coasts and in Europe. Nearly 60 cultivars of the Chisolm-Merritt (C.M.) hybrids were introduced around 1947 from Maryland. Coolidge (C) Gardens in California introduced nearly 50 in 1930. Another large group, the Yerkes-Pryor of Beltsville Hybrids (Bel.), have been developed primarily for forcing, but are of value outdoors. It would be impossible to give credit to all the hybridizers, but a list of some of the more common new Kurumes is as follows:

Addy Wery: flowers orange red, medium.
Adonis: flowers white, hose-in-hose.
China Girl (C.M.): flowers orange red, 2 inches.
Coralie (C): flowers rose, hose-in-hose.
Coral Sea (C.M.): flowers light coral pink.
Dorothy (C.M.): flowers light pink.
Eleanor Allan: flowers pink, medium low.
Eureka (Bel.): flowers pink, hose-in-hose, medium, spreading.
Geisha (C): flowers coral, hose-in-hose.
Glory: flowers peach pink, medium to tall.
Guy Yerkes (Bel.): flowers salmon pink, hose-in-hose.
Hahn's Red: flowers bright red.
Hershey's Red: flowers bright red, double.
Hershey's Salmon: flowers salmon.
Hexe: flowers crimson red, hose-in-hose, low to medium, dense.
H. H. Hume (Bel.): flowers white, hose-in-hose.
Hino-crimson: flowers crimson red, low to medium.
Orange Cup: flowers reddish orange, hose-in-hose.
May Glory: flowers red.
Mayo's Magic Lily: flowers light pink with petaloid sepals, distinct, late flowering.
Massasoit: flowers dark red.
Pink Progress: flowers pink.
Polar Bear: flowers white, hose-in-hose, upright.
Ruth May: flowers pink, white, fused, distinct.
Sherwoodi (Sherwood Orchid): flowers violet red, dark blotch.
Sherwood Red: flowers orange red, medium.
Shimmer: flowers rose pink.
Singing Fountain: flowers rose red.

Beltsville Dwarfs or Pryor Dwarfs have been developed from the Beltsville Hybrid program.

There were 19 true dwarfs named and introduced in 1960, but they are still rare in the nurseries. The names all depict dwarf or small size and they are excellent forcing plants, or container plants and bonsai subjects. A few of these are:

Boutonniere: flowers white, hose-in-hose.
Pinkette: flowers pink.
Salmon Elf: flowers salmon, hose-in-hose.
White Nymph: flowers white.

Kaempferi Hybrids: This group was developed in Europe around 1918 and later in the United States. The plants are hardier than Kurumes, from Zone 6 to Zone 8b, usually of a tall, upright habit, with flowers slightly larger than Kurumes. The kaempferi hybrids are crosses of *R. kaempferi* X Malvatica, and are often called Malvatica Hybrids in Holland. Malvatica is possibly a hybrid of Hinode-giri X Indica Alba, *(R. mucronulatum)*.

Alice: flowers salmon red.
Betty: flowers orange pink.
Cleopatra: flowers lilac rose.
Fedora: flowers deep pink.
Oberon: flowers light pink.
Willy: flowers bright pink.
Wilhelmina Vuyk (Palestrina): flowers white.

Gable Hybrids: These were developed by the late Joseph Gable, a rhododendron hybridizer at Stewartstown, Pennsylvania. They are considered the hardiest evergreen azaleas for Zone 6 and can be grown in Zone 8. Other hybrid groups include: Girard (Geneva, Ohio), Pride (Butler, Pennsylvania), Shammarello (S. Euclid, Ohio). A few of the Gable Hybrids are:

Cameo: flowers shell pink, hose-in-hose, late.
Campfire: flowers red, hose-in-hose, tall.
Elizabeth Gable: flowers rose, frilled, medium, spreading.
Herbert: flowers reddish violet, hose-in-hose, medium, spreading.
Indian Summer: flowers salmon pink, fall

flowering.

James Gable: flowers red, hose-in-hose.

Louise Gable: flowers violet red, semidouble, low spreading.

Margie: flowers deep pink, low plant, midseason.

Mary Dalton: flowers orange red, hose-in-hose, tall upright plant.

Polaris: flowers white with faint chartreuse throat, hose-in-hose.

Purple Splendor: flowers reddish violet, hose-in-hose, medium.

Rosebud: flowers rose, hose-in-hose, double, late.

Rose Greeley: flowers white, hose-in-hose, medium.

Stewartstonian: flowers bright clear red.

Pericat Hybrids: This group of greenhouse forcing azaleas, originated by Alphonse Pericat of Collingdale, Pennsylvania, is thought to be hybrids of Belgian Indian Hybrids and Kurume Hybrids. The plants are generally considered as hardy as most Kurumes from Zone 7 to Zone 9.

Dawn: flowers phlox pink with white center, hose-in-hose, 2 inches, medium, spreading, early midseason.

Gardenia Supreme: flowers white with chartreuse throat and violet red blotch, hose-in-hose, semidouble, 1½ inches, medium, early midseason.

Hampton Beauty: flowers carmine rose, partially petaloid, 2 inches, medium, early midseason.

Hiawatha: flowers rose red, hose-in-hose, medium.

Madam A. Pericat: similar to Dawn.

Mme. Alphonse Pericat: hybrid of Madame A. Pericat.

Pericat (Pericat Pink): flowers pink, hose-in-hose, 2 inches, medium, late.

Pericat Salmon: flowers hose-in-hose, double.

Pinocchio: flowers rose, double, medium, early midseason.

Sweetheart Supreme: flowers rose pink, dark blotch, hose-in-hose, semidouble, 1¾ inches, medium, midseason, tender in Zone 8.

Glenn Dale Hybrids: This large group was developed by the late B. Y. Morrison, formerly Director of the National Arboretum in Washington, D. C. This was one of the largest azalea breeding programs in the country. Over 70,000 seedlings were produced from a wide variety of crosses, and over 400 cultivars were named. One of the objectives was to produce large flowered azaleas hardy in and beyond the Washington, D. C. area.

The plants are extremely variable, from early to late flowering and from low compact to tall heights. There is a wide range of color in the large flowers including such variations as stripes, flecks, and variegated margins and throats. Many of the Glenn Dale and Satsuki azalea sports produce varied flower colors on the same plant. For propagation purposes and to retain the original color, these branch mutations should be cut out. In the garden, however, they often add to the general interest. Unfortunately, many of the cultivars are not available and can only be seen in a few of the large display gardens, such as the National Arboretum and others.

Representative cultivars of this large hybrid group, based on approximate season of bloom for Zone 7 through Zone 8 are as follows. The Glenn Dale azaleas are not common in the deep South and the coastal regions, Zones 9 and 10. They frequently start flowering in January and February, and never do produce a mass display of color as with the Southern Indian hybrids.

EARLY FLOWERING (LATE MARCH TO MID-APRIL)

Allure: flowers pale rose pink, 2½ inches, medium.

Dayspring: flowers shading to pale rose, pink margin, white center, 2 inches, medium.

Festive: flowers white, striped pale rose, 2 inches, medium.

Geisha: flowers white, flaked and striped purple, 1½ to 2 inches, medium.

Glee: flowers mallow purple, striped and flaked, 2 to 2½ inches, medium.

Refrain: flowers soft rose pink with white margin, hose-in-hose, 2 inches, medium to tall.

Scout: flowers peach pink, 2 inches, medium.

Suwanee: flowers rose pink, 3 inches, medium, mid-April.

Trouper: flowers Nopal Red, 1½ inches, medium.

Wildfire: flowers scarlet red, lighter throat, 2½ inches, medium.

MIDSEASON (MID-APRIL TO MID-MAY)

Ambrosia: flowers pale apricot, 2 inches, distinct, medium to tall.

Aphrodite: flowers soft rose pink, 2 inches, medium low.

Beacon: flowers scarlet, 2 inches, medium.

Boldface: flowers white with lavender margin, 3 inches, medium low.

Buccaneer: flowers orange red, dark blotch, 2 inches, medium, May.

Commando: flowers rose purple, 2 to 2½ inches, broad spreading.

Copperman: brilliant orange red, 3 inches, medium low, May.

Eucharis: flowers frilled white, chartreuse blotch, 3 inches, low, May.

Evensong: flowers rose, 2 inches, medium, late April.

Everest: flowers white, chartreuse blotch, 2 inches, early May.

Fashion: flowers orange red, hose-in-hose, 2 inches, medium, late April.

Glacier: flowers white, chartreuse throat, 2½ inches, medium, late April, good foliage.

Glamour: flowers rose red, 2½ inches,

medium.

Grace Freeman: flowers violet pink, 3½ to 4 inches, medium.

Greeting: flowers coral rose, 2 inches, medium, late April.

Helen Close: flowers white, 2½ to 3 inches, low dense.

Martha Hitchcock: flowers white with magenta pink margin, 3 inches, medium low, late April.

Muscadine: flowers rose purple, 3½ inches, medium.

Silver Mist: flowers white, sanded, flocked magenta, medium to low, May.

Surprise: flowers orange red, irregular white margin, 3 inches, medium, May.

Treasure: flower bud faint pink, open white with pink blotch, 3½ inches, medium tall, late April.

Trophy: flowers light pink, 3 inches, medium low, May.

Vestal: flowers white, chartreuse blotch, 2½ inches, medium, May.

Zulu: flowers purple, 3 to 3½ inches, medium.

LATE FLOWERING (MID-MAY TO JUNE)

Abbot: flowers rose red, 2½ to 3 inches, medium.

Angela Place: flowers white, 3 inches, low, spreading.

Aztec: flowers peach red, 3 inches, low, spreading.

Cremona: flowers vivid rose, 3 inches, medium low.

Chanticleer: flowers purple, 2 inches, medium.

Crusader: flowers light orange red, 2⅓ inches, low.

Crinoline: flowers rose pink, ruffled margin, 3 inches, medium.

Eros: flowers orange red, 3 inches, low.

Dauntless: flowers purple, 2 inches, low, dense.

Fawn: flowers white, light pink margin, 2½

inches, medium.

Jubilee: flowers Eosine Pink, 2½ inches, low.

Mary Helen: flowers white with chartreuse blotch, 2 inches, medium, spreading.

Meteor: flowers purple, 3 inches, broad, spreading.

Moonbeam: flowers white, frilled, 3 to 4 inches, medium.

Masquerade: flowers white, flaked and striped pink, 2½ inches, compact.

Janet Noyes: flowers brilliant rose, 2½ inches, medium, compact.

Pearl Bradford: flowers rose pink, 3 inches, low, spreading.

Sagittarius: flowers salmon pink, 3 inches, low, compact.

Sterling: flowers rose pink, 3 inches, low, spreading.

Sarabande: flowers white center, light purple margin, 3 inches, medium.

Swansong: flowers white with yellow blotch, 3 to 4 inches, medium.

Wavelet: flowers white with yellow blotch, 2½ inches, medium.

Back Acres Hybrids: This is a group of azaleas developed by the late B. Y. Morrison at Pass Christian, Mississippi, after his retirement from the National Arboretum. They are an extension of his Glenn Dale Azalea work with late flowering cultivars and plants with double flowers and multiple color forms. The plants are noted for their heavy, heat-resistant foliage and for their flowers of substance and texture. The plants should be rated with the Glenn Dales for cold resistance and are adaptable from Zone 7a to Zone 9a. Callaway Gardens was pleased to be one of the first to display this new group of hybrids, totaling 24, some still listed under numbers.

Eight cultivars of the original introduction are listed at present. The following plants are all midseason to late (mid-May in Georgia) and of medium height:

Debonaire: flowers light pink, nearly circular, 3 inches.

Margaret Douglas: flowers white to flush pink center, salmon pink margin, 3 inches.

Marion Lee: flowers white center, pink margin, 3 inches.

Pat Kraft: flowers scarlet red, 3 to 4 inches.

Saint James: flowers white throat, peach red margin, 3 inches.

Target: flowers scarlet, 3 inches.

Tharon Perkins: flowers pale salmon, 2 to 3 inches.

White Jade: flowers white, pale green throat, ruffled, 3 inches.

Satsuki Hybrids: Satsuki azaleas are of Japanese origin, prized for their large, single flowers and bonsai qualities.

Satsuki means Fifth Month, and the plants are late blooming, in May and early June. Many of the narrow-leaved evergreen plants are low growing or dwarf, while others will develop into medium to tall plants. The parentage of these hybrids is uncertain. They are possible variations of *R. indicum*, Indica or Macrantha azalea, the dwarf Indica azalea *(R. eriocarpum)* or hybrids between these and other cultivars. Included in the Satsukis will be found forms of *R. indicum*, such as the Macranthas and the Gumpo azaleas, which are included as a form of *R. eriocarpum.*

The Satsuki azaleas share a great variability in color and form, and they sport freely. Thus, a typical white flowered plant may appear flaked, margined, or colored, all on the same plant. The plants are slightly less hardy than the Kurumes, and are adaptable from Zone 7b to Zone 9a. They will grow in full sun, still, in the South, because of their late flowering, it is best to give protection from afternoon exposure.

There are several hundred cultivars, but many are known only in Japan and are rare in this country. It is unfortunate that the plants are not better known. They may be used in Southern gardens to extend the azalea flower season.

A list of some of the more common Satsukis, including forms of *R. indicum* and *R. eriocarpum*, is as follows:

Balsaminaeflorum (Rosaeflora), *R. indicum:* flowers orange red, very double, low, distinct.

Bene-kirin: flowers orange red, double, 2½ inches.

Bene-kirishima: flowers orange red, double, 2 inches.

Bunkwa (Bunka): flowers flesh pink to white, salmon pink margin.

Flame Creeper, *R. indicum:* flowers orange red, low, spreading.

Gumpo, *R. eriocarpum:* flowers white with occasional red flakes, frilled, 3 inches, compact, dense.
There are also Pink Gumpo, a light pink, and Red Gumpo, a salmon rose.

Gunrei: flowers white with pink flakes, 2 inches.

Gunbi: flowers white with red flecks, frilled, 2½ inches, low, spreading.

Gyokushin: flowers white with flush of pink, 3½ inches, low, spreading.

Ho-raku (How Raku): flowers white with flecks and sections rose red, low, spreading, extremely variable.

Jindai: flowers white, washed pink and pink flakes, 3 to 4 inches, late.

Keisetsu: flowers white, red margin or flecks, 2½ inches, low.

Kinghetsu: flowers white, rose stripes and flakes, 3½ to 4 inches.

Kow-koku: flowers white, red flecks, frilled, 3 inches, low, late.

Macrantha, *R. indicum:* flowers pink, 2½ inches, medium.
There is also Macrantha Red, a salmon red, and Macrantha Double.

Mai-hime: flowers pure rose to white or flecked, medium, extremely variable.

Okina-nishiki: flowers orange red, hose-in-hose, low, spreading.

Shinnyo-no-tsuki: flowers white, rose margin, large, 3 to 4 inches, low, spreading, tenderer than other Satsukis.

Waka-bisu: flowers salmon pink, hose-in-hose, 2½ inches, medium.

This concludes a brief discussion of the major azalea groups, omitting such names as Hirado, Wada, Hill, Yoder, and many others. Azalea breeders throughout the country are still active, and new cultivars, both for the home garden and for greenhouse forcing, will be forthcoming.

Evergreen Azalea Species: Before closing the discussion on evergreen azaleas, some of the more important evergreen species should be included.

R. kiusianum, Kyushu azalea: a small dense plant from the island of Kyushu, Japan. The leaves are small and deciduous in cooler climates. The flowers are small, purple to pink and rarely, white. The plant is frequently grown as a container plant or bonsai. Zone 7 to Zone 9a.

R. macrosepalum, Big sepal azalea: a native of Honshu and Shikoku, Japan. The flowers are 2 inches across and violet red. Zone 7 to Zone 8b.

R. macrosepalum linearifolium: a form with distinct narrow rose pink, strap-like petals. The form Seigai is distinct with long narrow leaves (¼ inch wide and ½ inch long) and narrow separate petals. Seigai is cold hardy from Zone 6 to Zone 8b, but may be nearly deciduous in colder climates, and have some flower bud damage. The plant is, however, of horticultural interest.

R. indicum and *R. eriocarpum* are late flowering evergreen species from Japan covered in the discussion on the Satsuki hybrids.

R. mucronatum, Azalea Indica Alba or Lediflora Alba: There is a question if this plant is a true species, having never been found in the wild, and yet known in Japanese gardens for hundreds of years. The azalea has several different names, Indica Alba and Lediflora Alba, and is often included with the Southern Indian Hybrids. The flowers are white, 3 inches, with slight fragrance. Plants are hardy from Zone 7a to Zone 9b and have taken an important place in the garden, flowering after the Kurume Snow, and in azalea hybridizing.

Several cultivars of *R. mucronatum* are also available:
Indica Rosea: flushed pink.
Lilacina: flowers lavender pink.
Delaware Valley White: flowering slightly earlier and with more compact form.
North Carolina White: very similar to Delaware Valley White and reputed to be hardy in Zone 6b.

R. poukhanense: a native of Korea and cold hardy from Zone 6 to Zone 8b, persistent-leaved species in the South, but may be deciduous in colder climates, as in Zone 6. The plant is of medium height and has fragrant reddish violet to pinkish flowers.

R. poukhanense yedoense, Yodogawa: a very double violet red form not found in the wild. Some botanists have given the double form a species rank, *R. yedoense,* and the single form as a variety.

R. serpyllifolium, Wild thyme azalea: is a small evergreen species (¼ inch wide and ½ inch long) with small light pink flower about ½ inch in size. There is a white flowered form, Albiflorum, more readily available from the west coast. The wild thyme azalea is native to the islands of Shiboku and Kyushu, Japan, and

hardy in Zone 6 to Zone 8b. The plant is extremely slow growing and is prized as a bonsai plant.

DECIDUOUS AZALEAS

NORTH AMERICAN SPECIES

Deciduous azaleas are valued by gardeners for their beautiful flowers. Colors of the flowers, include many tints and shades, ranging from white, yellow, orange, scarlet red, pink, and lavender. In addition to beautiful flowers, many species also have a delightful fragrance.

The most important group of deciduous azaleas are in the Luteum subseries which includes the fourteen species of native azaleas found in the eastern United States. The subseries Canadense, in addition to Japanese species, includes two species, *R. canadense* and *R. vaseyi* from the eastern United States. The flowers have very short tubes and appear bell shape with separate petals. Fortunately, our native azaleas are finally being recognized for their beauty and landscape value, and nurserymen are beginning to grow various species due to an ever increasing demand. The native azaleas have been called the most beautiful of all our indigenous shrubs, and in the past have received more praise from British and European gardeners than those in this country. Confusion of common names and misbeliefs follow the native azaleas. Often they have been called bush or wild honeysuckle when botanically they belong to the genus *Rhododendron.* It is interesting to note that some of the species were first discovered in the early 1700's by plant explorers. Yet, only in the twentieth century are they being recognized as handsome native plants and given an important place in the garden.

The native azaleas are deciduous. They lose their leaves during the winter which to many is objectionable, however, the ease of culture

R. viscosum, *Swamp Azalea*

and abundance of blooms outweighs this deficiency. The individual azalea flowers of the Luteum subseries are trumpet-shaped with five petals and a slender elongated corolla tube. Depending on species, the flowers are borne in few to large terminal clusters. On some, the flowers come before or with the new leaves, and on others, later after the leaves are fully developed.

The following description of native azalea species is according to the order of flowering as observed at Callaway Gardens. The sequence of flowering, however, may vary from year to year.

It should also be pointed out that the native azaleas are difficult to classify taxonomically because there is a great deal of similarity between various species. To add to the confusion, natural hybridization also occurs between species, resulting in many unusual and non-typical color variations.

Rhododendron canescens, Sweet, Piedmont or

Florida pinxter azalea, is the most abundant in the southeast, and its native range extends from north Florida to Texas, Alabama, Tennessee, Georgia, and North Carolina. The plant hardiness range is from Zone 9 to Zone 6b. Mark Catesby, the famed ornithologist, discovered the Piedmont azalea around 1730 on a trip to Florida and the Carolinas. The fragrant flowers, varying from white to light or deep pink, bloom before or with the new leaves in late March and early April. The plant is often a large shrub 10 to 15 feet in height and is found in diverse habitats along the streams, in moist woods, and on dry ridges. This species is generally not described as being stoloniferious (forming large colonies from underground shoots). However, stoloniferous forms are found and may be natural hybrids with either *R. viscosum* or *R. nudiflorum*. Those having a strong yellow blotch in the upper petal and other color variations may be intergrades with *R. austrinum*, *R. alabamense*, or *R. specosium*.

Rhododendron austrinum (Small) Rehder, Florida azalea, produces fragrant golden

64

R. bakeri, *Cumberland Azalea*

R. arborescens, *Sweet Azalea*

R. specosium, *Oconee Azalea*

R. alabamense, *Alabama Azalea*

R. austrinum, *Florida Azalea*

R. prunifolium, *Plumleaf Azalea*

R. canescens, *Piedmont Azalea*

R. vaseyi, *Pinkshell Azalea*

flowers in late March and early April along with the piedmont azalea. Like its allied plant, the flowers are borne before or with the new leaves. Although called Florida azalea, the native range of this species is from northern and western Florida to southwest Georgia, southern Alabama, and southeastern Mississippi. The hardiness range for the Florida azalea extends from Zone 9 to Zone 6b. This species was first discovered around 1815 by Dr. Chapman in northern Florida.

The general characteristics of this species, except for the beautiful yellow flowers, are very similar to those of the piedmont azalea. Both species are difficult to recognize when not in flower, because the pubescent or hairy underside of the foliage, and the soft gray pubescent floral buds are similar. The flowers range from a clear yellow to those having a pink or strawberry red tube as a result of interbreeding with the piedmont azalea.

Rhododendron specosium (flammeum, Wild) Sweet, Oconee azalea, with colorful flowers ranging from orange red, salmon to strong pink, and yellow, is one of the most attractive species in the South. Erroneously called flame azalea, it differs from *R. calendulaceum,* by its earlier flowering habit and its nonglandular flower tube. The nonfragrant flowers are normally borne in early to mid-April following the Piedmont azalea and before *R. alabamense.* The Oconee azalea is found in open woods and woody slopes in a band of the Piedmont region from eastern Alabama, across central Georgia to South Carolina. The hardiness range is not known but would include Zone 8b to Zone 6b. Andre Michaux, the famous French botanist, collected the plant in 1787 and compared the color of the flowers with *Hemerocallis fulva.* The plants vary from low mounding shrubs to 6 feet or more in height. Natural hybrids of Oconee and Piedmont azalea result in handsome, fragrant, strong pink flowering plants with a deep yellow blotch in the upper

65

petal. Hybrids with other species may also occur in some remote regions. It has been noted that *R. canescens, R. specosium, R. alabamense,* and *R. viscosum* have been found flowering together in a late cool spring season, and may account for many unusual and variable natural hybrids.

In central Georgia around Atlanta, the natural stands of Oconee azalea are becoming scarce, and protective measures are needed for its preservation.

R. alabamense Rehder, Alabama azalea, is a rare plant of dry open woodlands and rocky hill sites of north central Alabama and of isolated areas in west central Georgia. The hardiness range would include Zone 8b to Zone 6b. Typically, the species is a low stoloniferous plant 3 to 6 feet in height. It flowers from mid to late April several weeks after *R. canescens.* The flowers are white or white with a distinct yellow blotch, and have an attractive lemon fragrance. This azalea hybridizes readily with the piedmont azalea, producing bluish pink and white intergrades which often flower earlier than the typical species and are usually taller growing. These attractive hybrids cover a larger geographical area than the species from Alabama, Georgia, Mississippi, and Tennessee, and are generally grouped with *R. alabamense.* They fill the flowering gap between its two parents. Typical *R. alabamense* is rare, however, the hybrids mentioned above are found in some nurseries and are excellent plants for their fragrant flowers.

R. nudiflorium (L) Torrey, Pinxterbloom azalea, a cold hardy species ranging from Zone 8 to Zone 4, is found only in the northern-most areas of the South, in North Carolina and Tennessee, extending up into Ohio and northward to Massachusetts. The Pinxterbloom azalea forms colonies of stoloniferous plants, usually medium in height. Four to 6 feet is common, but they range from dwarf to tall shrubs. The sweet flowers open in mid-April and vary from white or pale pink to deep violet in color. This very hardy plant is commonly found in dry woods, and is useful for mass planting. John Bartram sent seed or plants of this azalea to Peter Collinson in England around 1734. The pinxterbloom, along with flame and swamp azalea, were used in the development of the Ghent hybrid azaleas.

R. roseum (Loisel) Rehder, Roseshell azalea, has a wide distribution from the open woods of the mountains of Virginia, west to Missouri, north to Indiana, Ohio, and into New England. The hardiness for this cold hardy species ranges from Zone 8 to Zone 4. It is usually found in association with the Pinxterbloom azalea. However, the forms of this species least contaminated by hybridization are found in the Blue Ridge Mountains of Virginia. This hardy plant is similar to the pinxterbloom, but usually is not stoloniferous. The undersides of the leaves are covered with a soft pubescense and the flower tubes are glandular in contrast to pinxterbloom. The rose pink to deep pink flowers are noted for their spicy clove scent.

R. vaseyi Gray, Pinkshell azalea, and Rhodora, *R. canadense* (L) Torrey, are unlike other native azaleas with two lipped flowers. The two lower flower lobes are wider than the other lobes, and are divided nearly to the base. Both of these species belong to the subseries Canadense, noted for their bell shape flowers with short tubes, rather than long funnel-shaped tubes. The numbers of stamens vary from five to seven in pinkshell azalea and up to ten in Rhodora, while most native azaleas have only five. Pinkshell azalea is a tall upright plant indigenous to the mountains of western North Carolina, usually found at elevations of 3,000 feet and above. It was first discovered in 1878 on Balsam Mountain in North Carolina by George Vasey. The attractive airy blossoms, borne in mid-April, are various shades of rose pink with a green throat and orange red dots at the base of the upper petals. A white flowered form, White Find, is also available. The pinkshell azalea, while from a restricted area, is adapted to a wide area from the cold climate of Massachusetts to the warm southern regions of Georgia and the lower South—Zone 8 to Zone 4.

Rhodora is native from the east coast of Labrador, Zone 3b, south to New Jersey, and while very hardy, is best adapted for a cold moist climate. This plant is commonly seen in Zones 6 and 7 in a cool moist garden. Rhodora flowers often appear before the pinkshell azalea in early spring and vary from rose purple to white and with ten stamens.

R. atlanticum (Ashe) Rehder, Coastal azalea, is native to the coastal plains from Delaware south to North and South Carolina. The hardiness range extends from Zone 8b to 6b. It is a low growing shrub, 1 to 3 feet, strongly stoloniferous in its habit of growth. The attractive fragrant flowers are white or white flushed with pale red, some with a distinct yellow blotch. Many of the forms have leaves that are glaucous, or whitish on the underside. It is extremely hardy and should be more frequently used in mass plantings. Coastal azalea is known to hybridize with many other native azaleas including *R. canescens* in the South and *R. nudiflorum* further north.

R. viscosum Torrey, Swamp azalea, is native to Alabama, Georgia, Tennessee, and north to Maine. John Bannister, an English missionary to Virginia, discovered the swamp azalea and the pinxterbloom azalea about 1690, and sent a drawing of the swamp azalea to London. John Bartram later sent seed or plants around 1734 to Peter Collinson in England. It is a dense, stoloniferous plant, that is typically 5 feet tall, however, taller upright forms are also found. The slender tubed flowers are distinct, white to creamy white, with a strong spicy fragrance. The corolla tubes are notably glandular and quite sticky to the touch. The fragrant flowers are borne in mid-May to early June. At high elevations the plant is often a low mounding shrub and yet, along moist streams, it can be unusually tall. It is often found in pink forms, which are possible hybrids with *R. arborescens*. Hybrids with *R. calendulaceum*, the flame azalea, produce shades of color from pink to salmon yellow. Swamp azalea is useful in the home landscape for its fragrant white flowers, and hardy from Zone 9a to Zone 4a.

R. calendulaceum (Michaux) Torrey, Flame azalea, is claimed by many plant authorities to be one of the most beautiful native shrubs. The plant is indigenous to the Appalachian Mountain region from north Pennsylvania and Ohio south to north Georgia. William Bartram, the famous Philadelphia botanist, discovered the flame azalea in 1774 on the hillsides near the converging of the Savannah and Broad rivers in northeast Georgia, the most southern part of its range. Bartram described its beauty in his book, *Travels* (1790):

"The epithet fiery, I annex to this most celebrated species of azalea, as being expressive of the appearance of its flowers which are in general of the colour of the finest red lead, orange, and bright gold, as well as yellow and cream colour; these various splendid colours are not only in separate plants, but frequently all the varieties and shades are seen in separate branches on the same plants; and the clusters of the blossoms cover the shrub in such incredible profusion on the hillsides, that suddenly opening to view from dark shades, we were alarmed with the apprehension of the hill being set on fire. This is certainly the most gay and brilliant flowering shrub yet known."

The tall erect plants with spreading branches are found on open hillsides and along mountain streams. The flame azalea is noted for its large flowers which average nearly 2 inches across. The size of the flowers is associated with its tetraploid condition, that is, having twice the number of chromosomes as other species. Some plants may start flowering in early May while others flower later in mid- to late June. The flowers possess a beautiful diverse range in color from orange red, orange, to distinct clear yellow with an orange blotch. The dark orange to orange red phases are usually associated with plants from high elevations. The nonfragrant flowers are generally glandular on the flower tube, as contrasted with the nonfragrant Oconee azalea which is typically nonglandular.

The flame azalea is frequently used as a landscape plant in the northeast and should be used in the South. The plant is adaptable from Zone 8b to Zone 5a. When grown well, it is a handsome plant noted for its late flowering.

Rhododendron arborescens (Pursh) Torrey, Sweet azalea, is one of the best of the native white azaleas. It is generally found along streams and on moist mountain tops in Alabama, Georgia, Kentucky, Tennessee, and northward into Pennsylvania and New York.

Andre Michaux, the famous French botanist, observed the plant in 1795 on the Blue Ridge Mountains of North Carolina. The sweet azalea was later discovered by John or William Bartram and introduced by them to England. It is generally a tall upright growing plant reaching 6 to 10 feet in height, or even nearly small tree form as described by its species name, arborescens (treelike). The flowers are pure white, occasionally with a pink or reddish flush, and often with a prominent yellow blotch on the upper petal. The red style of the flower is eminently conspicuous against the white petals. The attractive fragrant flowers have a delightful heliotrope scent. The plant has a more lustrous glossy foliage than most species and a pleasant fragrance even when dried.

This species is hardy and reliable in moist areas. The plants are adapted from Zones 8b to 5a. The sweet azalea is a good landscape plant with good foliage and late fragrant flowers. The species is variable however, and there are some poor forms with small inferior flowers which are not very showy. Typically, sweet azalea blooms in late May and early June. However, a late flowered form has been found in the South that appears in July and occasionally on into August. The plant has been confused with the swamp azalea. However, the stems are smooth and nonhairy, as contrasted with the swamp azalea which has pubescent stems. The sweet azalea often hybridizes with the swamp azalea, producing attractive pink flowered forms. Occasionally, rare yellow flowered forms of sweet azalea are found.

Rhododendron oblongifolium Small, Texas azalea, is the most western species of the eastern natives, occurring in open woodlands, hills, and along streams in southwestern Arkansas to east Texas and Oklahoma. The fragrant white flowers appear in late April and May after the leaves are fully formed. *R. oblongifolium* is very similar to the swamp azalea, *R. viscosum,* and could be classified as a form of swamp azalea rather than a separate species. The plant has not been extensively tried in the garden and warrants further study.

R. bakeri, (Lemon & McKay) Hume, Cumberland azalea, was first described in 1937 from plants found in north Georgia by W. P. Lemon and McKay and named in honor of Dr. Woolford Baker, Professor emeritus of Emory University. In 1941 a red azalea found in the Cumberland Mountains of Kentucky was described by Dr. E. Lucy Braum and named *R. cumberlandense.* While there is still some disagreement, the two species are usually combined under the species, *R. bakeri,* or Cumberland azalea. The plants are generally found in open woods, usually at high elevations of the Cumberland Plateau in Kentucky,

Tennessee, to the mountains of north Georgia and Alabama. The plant is variable in height, ranging from low forms, 1 to 2 feet, to a medium height of 5 feet, or even higher, 6 to 10 feet. The flowers are similar to those of the flame azalea but with a narrower tube and flowering two or more weeks later than the flame azalea. The color ranges from orange, orange red, to red. Lighter colors of yellow to salmon are found in the southern range of Georgia and Alabama. A color phase named Camps Red is known from the summit of Big Black Mountain in Kentucky. The late Dr. Wendell Camp, a renowned botanist and horticulturist, was among the first to recognize the distinctiveness of the red azalea of the Cumberland Plateau and the name Camps Red now is used to designate a select form in his honor. Dr. Camp was so impressed with the beauty of the Cumberland azalea and described it in glowing words:

"Predominately they were red, a warm glowing, living red. The only way I can get the idea across is to have you imagine that you had an azalea with a warm lemon-yellow color. Now, dip it in scarlet, and it turns orange, a warm orange, much warmer than scarlet alone. Now, dip it again and again in the scarlet, and with each dipping, shift the color toward a deeper shade until it is a black red. That is the color of many of the plants. Some haven't been dipped so often — these are a startling contrast — but the majority are deep red — a warm, living, flashing red — and just as red in the forest as on the open meadows at the top of the mountains."

R. bakeri is thought to produce hybrids with *R. arborescens* and other species, adding to the interesting color forms that are found in the wild. The Cumberland azalea is still not readily available, but is certainly worthy of extensive trials in the home landscape for the late orange to orange-red flowers. The hardiness range is similar to the flame azalea

from Zone 8b to Zone 5b.

Plants of a single colony in north Georgia described as *R. furbishi* are regarded as a hybrid between a late *R. calendulaceum* form or *R. bakeri* and *R. arborescens,* rather than a distinct species.

R. serrulatum (Small) Millais, Hammock-sweet azalea, is a native of the wooded swamps of the Southern Coastal Plains from east central Georgia to central Florida, west to Mississippi and Louisiana. It was originally included with *R. viscosum* and is still often confused with the latter. *R. serrulatum* generally is a taller plant with brown-red flaring branches and later flowers than *R. viscosum.* The fragrant white flowers are borne in late July and August and have a long viscid or sticky glandulous tube. A fragrance of the flower is often described as clover-scented. *R. serrulatum* was first collected around 1830 near New Orleans, Louisiana, and in Florida. It was later introduced into cultivation by the Arnold Arboretum in 1919 from seed collected near Folkston, Georgia. Its hardiness is not generally known, but is valuable in Southern gardens for its late fragrant flowers. The hardiness range is from Zones 9a to 7a.

Rhododendron prunifolium, Plumleaf or "prunifolia" azalea, is restricted to southwestern Georgia and eastern Alabama, in shady ravines and along stream banks. It is a very distinct species with its glabrous or smooth stem and the late red flowers. It is a large shrub, often 15 to 20 feet in height, flowering after the leaves are fully developed. The nonfragrant flowers stand out in contrast to the dark green foliage. The flower color varies from orange, orange red, to red. Mr. Cason J. Callaway, founder of Callaway Gardens, received in 1947 the "Frances K. Hutcheson Award for Conservation", from the Garden Clubs of America for his efforts toward conservation, preservation, and perpetuation of this species. The extensive plantings of prunifolia azalea at the Gardens start flowering in early July, and there are spasmodic blooms on individual plants until late August and occasionally into early September. Many of the flower buds are candy striped, and have an unusual appearance, a condition observed with other species. The plumleaf azalea is an important garden plant for its late flowers and its hardiness in areas north of its native range. The adaptable hardiness range as known now is from Zone 9a to Zone 6b. As with other late flowering azaleas, it should be used in a shady area, particularly out of the afternoon sun. The plumleaf azalea was first collected by the late Alabama botanist Dr. R. M. Harper in 1903, and was later introduced into cultivation through the Arnold Arboretum in 1918.

Rhododendron coryi, Shinners, is a rare species that has been reported from only three counties (Tyler, Warren and Hardin) of southeast Texas. Specimens of this new azalea were first collected in 1950 by the late Dr. Victor L. Cory, of Southern Methodist University. While this new and rare species is not generally known to gardeners at the present, it should be extensively tested and evaluated throughout the South. Presently, this species is reported to bloom in southeast Texas in April after the leaves have developed; the flowers are white and probably fragrant. The plant is a low shrub 3 feet or less in height, stoloniferous, and is described as a dwarf form of *Rhododendron viscosum*.

Discussion of the native azaleas would not be complete without mentioning the western or Pacific azalea, *R. occidentale* Gray. While it is said to be similar to the flame azalea, it has its own distinct characteristics, and is certainly geographically disjunct from other azalea species. The Pacific azalea is distributed along mountain streams from southern Oregon to southern California in varying altitudes over 5,000 feet. The large late fragrant flowers vary from creamy white to pink with a distinct yellow blotch.

Gardeners are generally unsuccessful in growing *R. occidentale* in the East or the South, and that is often attributed to the warm humid summer weather in the East. Ross Nelson, of San Antonio, Texas, reported recently that he has succeeeded in growing the Pacific azalea in his area. Most Eastern and Southern growers find the plant seldom survives more than one or two years.

ASIAN AND EUROPEAN DECIDUOUS AZALEAS

R. flavum (luteum) Sweet, azalea lutea of Pontic azalea, the only azalea native to Europe, is found in the Caucasus-Black Sea region and northeast to Lithuania and Poland. It resembles *R. austrinum,* Florida azalea, in growth habit and in bright yellow, fragrant flowers. This species, along with many American species, was used in developing the Ghent azaleas. *R. flavum* is hardy to Zone 7 and is occasionally seen in the cooler areas of the South. It is generally not considered satisfactory for areas of long hot summer weather.

R. japonicum (Gray) Suringan, Japanese azalea, is common in open grassy areas on Honshu, Kyushu, and Shikoku, the main islands of Japan. The large flowers, up to 2 inches wide, vary from clear yellow, to orange red, to red. Its color range is similar to *R. specosium* and *R. calendulaceum.* It is hardy in Zone 6 and, while not extensively tried in the South, has proven adaptable around Atlanta, Georgia — Zone 8a.

R. molle (Bl.) G. Don, Chinese azalea, is a native of eastern and central China. This plant is less hardy than *R. japonicum* and is seldom seen in the South. The flowers are typically yellow to yellow orange, and its leaves have a whitish pubescence beneath. It has been used with *R. japonicum* to produce the Mollis hybrids.

R. pentaphyllum, Maxim, Fiveleaf-azalea, is noted for its whorls of five leaves at the end of branches. It has been confused with *R. quinquefolium* which also has whorled leaves. The plant is a large shrub or a small tree, and the large pink flowers appear before the leaves. This plant, while hardy in Zone 7, is rare in American gardens, however, it is worthy of trial and testing.

R. schlippenbachi Maxim, Royal azalea, is a native of Korea and northeastern Manchuria and is grown sparingly in central Japan. When grown well, the Royal azalea is one of the finest deciduous azaleas. It often is eccentric and slow to establish itself well. It is hardy in Zone 5 and is doing well at Callaway Gardens, Zone 8b. The large pink fragrant flowers with a brown dotted throat open in early spring as the leaves are expanding. The broad distinct obovate leaves are in whorls of five at the end of branches. There is also a white flowered form.

R. quinquefolium Biss and Moore, Cork azalea, is a native of central Japan. It resembles *R. pentaphyllum* with its whorled leaves, but is easily distinguished by its white rather than pink flowers. While rare in America, it is hardy in Zone 6 and should be tested in other areas.

There are other deciduous azaleas. Additional testing throughout the United States is required to learn of their adaptabilities. These include *R. albrechti, R. mareisi, R. nipponicum, R. reticulatum, R. weyrichi* to name a few.

HYBRID DECIDUOUS AZALEAS
From the palate of the many handsome deciduous azalea species, the azalea breeder began to develop new hybrids. This work started in the early 1800's in Europe, and is continuing still today throughout the world. Many of these hybrid groups were developed for cooler regions and have not been extensively tested in the South. It has also been found that while many of the selected named cultivars are not heat tolerant, the seedlings of these plants are. Thus, general information on these hybrid groups is important, and hopefully more people will test and evaluate these plants, reporting on their successes or failures.

Before leaving the deciduous azaleas, there is one plant considered by gardeners as a very early lavender azalea. This is *R. mucronulatum* Turez., Korean rhododendron of the daurian series. While it is deciduous and a true rhododendron, it is still referred to and included by many gardeners as an azalea. This species is noted for its very early lavender or pink flowers. It is hardy in Zone 5, and in many areas it is in flower with forsythia. It needs further trial in the deep South where it has been noted in some areas to flower during a period of early warm weather and then be killed back by a late spring freeze. A clear pink form is known as Cornell Pink and does well in Richmond, Virginia, and in other Southern areas, such as Callaway Gardens.

GHENT HYBRIDS
The Ghent hybrid azaleas were started in the 1820's by P. Mortier, a baker of Ghent, Belgium. The Ghent hybrids resulted from crossing crossing the European azalea, *R. flavum*, with North American species, *R. calendulaceum, R. nudiflorum, R. specosium,* and *R. viscosum.*

The Ghent hybrids are tall, upright plants flowering early to midseason. The flowers, both single and double, are 1½ to 2½ inches wide and vary from white to yellow through orange to red. The plants are very hardy to Zone 5 and prefer a cool climate. Very few of the many named cultivars are adapted to the warmer climates.

Seedlings of Ghent hybrids and of the other hybrid groups are generally preferred in the warmer climates.

Two Ghent hybrids doing well at Callaway Gardens are:
1) Daviesi: a tall plant with pale yellow or white flowers, 2¼ inches in size, described as a viscosepalum hybrid. *(R. molle* x viscosum).
2) Narcissiflora: a tall plant with sweet scented, double yellow flowers.

MOLLIS HYBRIDS
The Mollis hybrids were developed in the late 1880's in Belgium from crosses of *R. japonicum* x *R. molle* with some swamp azalea genes. The Mollis hybrids are less hardy than the Ghents and are thought to be more heat resistant, however, this has not been proven by evaluating varieties throughout the South.

Two varieties known to do well in Zone 8 are:
1) Hugo Koster: large reddish orange flowers, 2¾ inches with an orange blotch.
2) J. C. van Tol: large orange-red flowers, 2¾ inches with a yellowish blotch.

KNAPHILL HYBRIDS
In England, the more recent developments of the Ghent and Mollis hybrids introduced after World War II are classified under the name Knaphill. The large flowers, 2 to 3 inches wide, are flat, thickly textured, and vary in many fine shades of color from near white to cream, pink, orange, and red.

The Knaphill strain originated at the Waterer's Knaphill Nursery. Later the Slocock's developed additional hybrids in the Goldsworth Old Nursery in England. Work was still carried forward by the late Edgar Stead at the Island Estate in Christchurch, New Zealand, and by the late Lionel de Rothschild at Exbury, Southhampton, in England. Thus, there are four subgroups of the Knaphill hybrids: the

R. calendulaceum, *Flame Azalea*

R. canescens, *Piedmont Azalea.*

R. alabamense, *Alabama Azalea*

Knaphill, Slocock, Ilam, and Exbury selections. There are also new Knaphill Hybrids constantly being introduced from Europe and in this country. Many nurseries are finding these azaleas difficult to propagate asexually by cuttings, and are selling seedlings from types that produce rather consistent colors. The Ilam hybrids have been reported to be heat resistant, however, on limited tests at Callaway Gardens this has not been true with all cultivars.

Throughout the South, the Knaphill hybrid azalea seedlings are proving better than the named cultivars. In the cooler regions of the South, the Knaphill hybrids will become more popular. Hopefully, Southern azalea breeders will continue to work with this group of large-flowered azaleas and the heat tolerant native species to develop new heat tolerant cultivars.

Hybrid and Evergreen Rhododendrons

Interest in the evergreen and hybrid rhododendrons is steadily increasing in the South. The southern Appalachians are the home of four native evergreen species: *R. catawbiense, R. carolinianum, R. maximum* and *R. minus,* while *R. chapmani* is a native of the coastal plain, pine hills country of northwestern Florida. Many people make annual visits to see the native rhododendron display in the mountain habitats at Craggy Gardens, Grandfather Mountain, Mount Pisgah, and Mount Mitchell in North Carolina, to Roan Mountain and the Great Smoky Mountain areas of Tennessee such as Newfound Gap and Clingmans Dome, or to Brasstown Bald in Georgia. Viewing the natives and then the hybrid rhododendrons in eastern and western gardens has developed the challenge to grow evergreen rhododendrons in the South. The Southern gardeners in Zone 6 will find they can grow most rhododendron cultivars that have been proven hardy in the East. Gardeners in Zone 7 become more selective and the real challenge is for the gardeners in Zone 8.

Before going any further, we will review the native rhododendrons.

R. catawbiense Michaux. Catawba rhododendron is a plant of the high mountains (usually 3,000 feet and above) of the southern Alleghenies from West Virginia to Georgia and Alabama. It develops into a shrub of 6 to 8 feet in height, and occasionally higher. The shiny dark evergreen leaves are 3 to 6 inches long, and are pale whitish beneath. The flowers are borne in clusters or rounded trusses in May and June before new growth develops. The individual flowers are bell shape, usually 2 inches across, and lilac-magenta spotted with olive green in the throat. It is one of the best known of the native rhododendrons, and is considered one of America's finest native shrubs in spite of its purplish flowers. White flowered forms have also been found, and two white cultivars are Glass and Catalgla.

Catawba rhododendron is hardy in Zone 5 to Zone 7 and adapted to the cooler regions of Zone 8a. Unfortunately, thousands of these plants are grown or collected and sold in cities of low elevation only to barely exist and slowly die after several years. Southern rhododendron enthusiasts are now interested in growing seedlings of *R. catawbiense insulare,* a low elevation variety found in restricted areas in Georgia and North Carolina at 300 to 900 feet. It is hoped that seedlings of this low elevation type will be available to Southern gardeners in the near future.

R. maximum L. Rosebay rhodendron is a large spreading shrub 6 to 12 feet in height. In the Appalachian Mountains it may become a small tree, 35 feet high. Its natural range extends from Nova Scotia, Ontario, Ohio, and southward through the Alleghenies from New York to Georgia and Alabama. The narrow dark evergreen leaves are 4 to 10 inches long, and are usually glabrous and pale beneath. The individual flowers, 1½ inches across, are pale rose or nearly white with green to yellowish spots in the upper petal. The plant blooms in June to July after the new growth has developed. Both a pure white and a pinkish red flowered form have been found. Rosebay rhododendron is hardy in Zone 4 to Zone 8, and while it has limited use in the landscape due to its large size, it is generally more heat tolerant than the Catawba rhododendron.

In the mountains, both of these species are often referred to as "laurel". A "laurel slick" is a mountain side of rhododendron. In the same regions, mountain laurel, *Kalmia latifolia,* is mistakenly called "ivy".

Rhododendron carolinianum Rehder, Carolina rhododendron usually is a compact shrub less than 6 feet tall with glossy evergreen leaves, 2 to 3 inches long. The rose purple to white flowers are 1½ inches across, and are borne in small clusters in May. There is a white

R. minus, *Piedmont Rhododendron*

Album Elegans, *Hybrid Rhododendron*

flowered variety, R, *c. album,* Carolina rhododendron which is hardy from Zones 5 to 7b, and is native in the Blue Ridge Mountains of the Carolinas and Tennessee.

Rhododendron minus Michaux, Piedmont rhododendron has a more open habit of growth and is taller than the Carolina rhododendron. It is a loose shrub which grows up to 10 feet tall and has evergreen leaves 2 to 4 inches long. The flowers appear in late May after the Carolina rhododendrons, and are pink to magenta to rose pink. The plant is found at lower mountain elevations from North Carolina to Georgia and Alabama. Natural hybrids occur between the Carolina and Piedmont rhododendrons. The Piedmont rhododendron is hardy from Zone 5 to Zone 8.

Rhododendron chapmani Gray, Chapman's rhododendron is found far south of the Blue Ridge Mountains in the coastal plains region of northwestern Florida. This restricted species is found in the sandy pine forest at low elevations and is very drought tolerant. The plant is upright, spreading in habit of growth and is 6 to 8 feet tall with oval glossy evergreen foliage 2 to 3 inches long. Its hardiness is not completely known, but it is believed to range from Zone 5 to Zone 9a. The clear pink to rose pink flowers appear in May. Chapman and Piedmont rhododendrons are described by some botanists as only varieties of *R. carolinianum.* However, I prefer to classify them as species. The foliage of both the Carolina and Piedmont rhododendron has a reddish cast in the winter, while the Chapman rhododendron foliage usually remains green. Chapman rhododendron seedlings are now available from nurserymen and should become better known by Southern gardeners.

In most gardens the hybrid rhododendrons are used more frequently than the species. Hybrid rhododendrons are generally more floriferous and adaptable to garden conditions. Both, however, have their particular value.

The hybrid craze began in England in the early 1800's when Michael Waterer, an English nurseryman, crossed two imported species, *R. maximum* and *R. catawbiense,* both native to North America.

As the interest in rhododendrons developed, the exploration and search for new species continued with such men as Sir Joseph Hooker, Robert Fortune, Ernest Wilson, J. F. Rock, and F. Kingdom-Ward. Today, over 900 species rhododendron and 8,000 hybrids have been recorded.

When selecting a rhododendron hybrid for a Southern garden, there are some factors to consider, including hardiness of adaptability and heat tolerance.

Most species and hybrids are rated by the American Rhododendron Society for cold hardiness. We found in the South that the ratings only serve as a guide because many plants are injured at temperatures higher than those indicated by their rating. For example, a plant which has a hardiness rating of H-3 may be injured at a temperature of +5°F. or higher.

A.R.S. - HARDINESS RATING

H-1	Hardy to −25°F below Zero
H-2	Hardy to −15°F
H-3	Hardy to − 5°F
H-4	Hardy to + 5°F
H-5	Hardy to +15°F
H-6	Hardy to +25°F
H-7	Hardy to +32°F

Based on this system, at Callaway Gardens we should be able theoretically to grow plants rated as H-4, however, we find that this is not always the case. We depend more on the extremely cold hardy types in H-1 and H-2 and, occasionally, in H-3. This has been observed in other areas of the South and is due to our fluctuating winter temperatures. A warm period in mid-winter may initiate plant growth only to be followed by a sudden drop in temperature, resulting in plant damage that may not show up until spring.

Planting to avoid winter sun and the coolest site aids the plant in remaining dormant.

Heat tolerance in the South is even less understood than cold hardiness. The elevation above sea level has been found to be fortunate in determining what cultivars or hybrids to plant. At 2,000 feet or higher, many varieties will withstand full open summer sun. Below 1,000 feet elevation, light to medium shade is preferred, preferably avoiding noon and afternoon sun.

It is interesting that many of the extremely cold hardy cultivars are also the most heat tolerant. In 1926, Ernest Wilson, the noted plant explorer, published a list of very hardy rhododendrons which became known as the "ironclad" hybrids. Even today many of these old cultivars are still important plants for the Southern garden. Some cultivars will frequently flower in the early fall in the lower South and thus are not recommended.

The culture of rhododendrons is similar to azaleas and the same general recommendations can be followed. Rhododendrons are troubled with several root rot fungi, and for this reason the basic plant requirements must be met.

Rhododendron cultivars in the past were propagated by grafting. However, with the new techniques of propagation, most of them are available as rooted cuttings, and only rooted plants should be used. Species rhododendrons are often only available as seedlings, however, some of the better selections are also grown from cuttings.

A list of some of the rhododendron cultivars and species for the South is included. Rhododendron gardeners will also gain a great deal of assistance from a local chapter of the American Rhododendron Society.

RHODODENDRON SPECIES

SPECIES	ARS HARDINESS	Sun 2000' and above	Shade below 2000'	Shade below 1000'	Remarks
Rhododendron carolinianum Carolina Rhododendron	H-1	X	X		rosy pink, loose to compact
Rhododendron catawbiense Catawba Rhododendron	H-1	X	X		high elevations
R. catawbiense insulare	H-2		X	X	found at low elevations
Rhododendron chapmani Chapman Rhododendron	H-3		X	X	rose pink flowers, heat tolerant
Rhododendron fortunei Fortunes Rhododendron	H-2	X shade	X	X	fragrant pink flowers
Rhododendron keiskei Keisk Rhododendron	H-2	X shade	X	?	yellow flowers, dwarf
Rhododendron maximum Rosebay Rhododendron	H-1	X	X	X	pinkish white flowers, large shrub
Rhododendron micranthum Manchurian Rhododendron	H-2				small white flowers, and small leaves
Rhododendron minus Piedmont Rhododendron	H-2	X	X	X	pink flowers, open, upright
Rhododendron yakusimanum Yak Rhododendron	H-2	X	X	X	pink to white flowers, compact shrub, many new hybrid forms

RHODODENDRON CULTIVARS
WHITE

CULTIVARS	ARS HARDINESS	Sun 2000' and above	Shade below 2000'	Shade below 1000'	Remarks
x Album Elegans	H-1	X	X	X	tall, hardy plant
x Boule de Neige	H-1	X	X	X	pure white flowers, hardy
x Catawbiense Album	H-1	X	X	X	hardy, good grower
Cunningham White	H-2	X	X	?	greenish blotch, tough
Dora Amateis	H-2		X	X	semi-dwarf, leaves 3″
x Gomer Waterer	H-2	X	X	X	rose pink buds, late flowering

PINK

CULTIVARS	ARS HARDINESS	Sun 2000' and above	Shade below 2000'	Shade below 1000'	Remarks
Amy	H-3		X	X	vigorous
Anna Rose Whitney	H-3		X	X	vigorous grower
Cynthia	H-3	X	X	X	rose red
English Roseum	H-1	X	X	X	easy to grow
x Everestianum	H-1	X	X	X	lavender pink
Holden	H-1	X	X		rose red
Jan Deken	H-3		X	X	ruffled pink flowers
P.J.M.	H-1	X	X	?	flowers in the fall in zone 8, foliage 3"
x Roseum Elegans	H-1	X	X	X	mauve pink, easy to grow
Scintillation	H-2	X	X	X	good foliage

RED

CULTIVARS	ARS HARDINESS	Sun 2000' and above	Shade below 2000'	Shade below 1000'	Remarks
x America	H-1	X	X	X	small dark red flowers
x Charles Dickens	H-1	X	X	X	crimson purple
Jean Marie de Montague	H-3		X	X	brilliant red, compact growth
x Nova Zembla	H-1	X	X	X	dark red flowers, good grower
Vulcan	H-3		X	X	bright red

BLUE-PURPLE

CULTIVARS	ARS HARDINESS	Sun 2000' and above	Shade below 2000'	Shade below 1000'	Remarks
A. Bedford	H-3	X	X	X	light blue, purple center
Blue Peter	H-2	X	X	X	light lavender blue flowers
Caroline	H-2	X	X	?	fragrant orchid lavender flowers
Lee's Dark Purple	H-2	X	X		flowers in the fall in zone 8

x—"ironclad"

Recommended List of Evergreen and Deciduous Azaleas

There are several thousands of azalea cultivars named and described. Unfortunately, in many areas of the country less than 50 cultivars are commonly available.

The list of azaleas is by hardiness zones along with varieties generally available for a given area. Evergreen varieties listed for Zone 6 to 7b will generally be adapted for the warmer zones and many of the varieties listed for Zone 8b to 9 are considered tender varieties and are generally not recommended for cooler areas.

Key:

BA	Back Acres hybrid	GH	Ghent hybrid	M	*R. mucronatum* cv.
BH	Belgian hybrid	I	*R. indictum* cv.	P	Pericat hybrid
G	Gable hybrid	K	Kurume hybrid	R	Rutherford hybrid
GD	Glenn Dale hybrid	KA	Kaempferi hybrid	S	Satsuki hybrid
		KH	Knaphill hybrid	SI	Southern Indian hybrid

RECOMMENDED LIST OF DECIDUOUS AZALEAS

The deciduous azaleas, except for the native azalea, in general are not as common or known in the South. The natives are listed as being adapted throughout the hardiness zones from Zone 7 to Zone 9. More care and selection of site will be required in the warmer areas such as in Zone 9.

The Ghent, Mollis, and Exburys will be found adaptable in the cooler zones such as Zones 6 and 7. It has been noted that more seedlings of this type are available and adaptable than the named cultivars.

More testing and evaluation of these types are needed in the warmer areas included in Zones 8 and 9.

DECIDUOUS AZALEAS ZONE 6 to 8a

White
> *R. canescens* (clones)   *R. viscosum*   *R. arborescens*
> *R. vaseyi*, White Find   *R. atlanticum*
> *R. alabamense* (clones)   Daviesi (GH)

Pink
> *R. canescens*   *R. nudiflorum*
> *R. vaseyi*   *R. roseum*
>   Cecile (KH)

Yellow-Orange-Orange Red-Red
> *R. austrinum*   *R. calendulaceum*   *R. bakeri*
> *R. specosium* (clones)   Narcissiflora (GH)   *R. prunifolium*
>   *Pallas (GH)*
>   *Exbury hybrids*

Lavender
> *R. poukhanense*   *R. mucronulatum*

DECIDUOUS AZALEAS ZONE 8b to 9

White

R. canescens (clones)   *R. viscosum*   *R. arborescens*
R. vaseyi, White Find   Daviesi (GH)   *R. serrulatum*
R. alabamense (clones)

Pink

R. canescens   *R. nudiflorum*
R. vaseyi   *R. roseum*

Yellow-Orange-Red

R. austrinum   *R. calendulaceum*   *R. bakeri*
R. specosium (clones)   Exbury hybrids   *R. prunifolium*
                            Ilam hybrids*

* for evaluation

DECIDUOUS AZALEAS ZONE 9a to 9b

Compiled by Dr. Sigmond L. Solymosy, University of Southwestern Louisiana

White

R. canescens (clone)   *R. oblongifolium*   *R. coryi*
R. alabamense (clone)   *R. viscosum glaucum*

Pink

R. canescens   *R. nudiflorum*   *R. serrulatum* (clone)

Yellow-Orange-Red

R. austrinum   *R. austrinum* (clones)   *R. prunifolium* (clones)
R. specosium (clones)   *R. calendulaceum* (clones)

80

Bridesmaid Azalea

Coral Bells Azalea

Redwings Azalea

Hino Azalea   *Gloria Azalea*

George Lindley Taber

Johga Azalea

Ruth May Azalea

R. serpyllifolium, *Wild Thyme Azalea*

Glacier Azalea

Margaret Douglas Azalea

Koromo-shikibu Azalea

Criterion Azalea

EVERGREEN AZALEAS FOR ZONE 6a to 7b

The first group of azaleas for Zone 6a to 7b was compiled and modified from an article by Franklin H. West, M.D., Gladwyne, Pennsylvania, "On the Azalea Inferiority Complex and Rhododendronitis", Vol. 27, 1973, American Rhododendron Society, Quarterly Bulletin.

White

Early	Midseason	Late
Rose Greely (G)	Delaware Valley White (M)	Gumpo (S)
Polaris (G)	Glacier (GD)	Everest (GD)
Wilhelmina Vuyk (KA)	Treasure (GD)	Swansong (GD)
Snow (K)	Helen Close (GD)	Wavelet (GD)

White (Variegated, striped and bordered)

Geisha (GD)	Martha Hitchcock (GD)	Kinghetsu (S)
Delight (GD)	Surprise (GD)	Gyokushin (S)
Refrain (GD)	Boldface (GD)	Jindai (S)

Orange Red–Orange Pink

Mary Dalton (G)	Copperman (GD)	Balsaminaeflorum (I)
Addy Wery (K)	Stewartstonian (G)	Beni-kirishima (S)
Coral Bells (Kirin) (K)	Fashion (GD)	Flame Creeper (I)
Sherwood Red (K)	Greeting (GD)	

Rose Red

Campfire (G)	Elizabeth Gable (G)	Aztec (GD)
Hino-crimson (K)	Margie (G)	Mai-hime (S)
James Gable (G)	Glamour (GD)	Pearl Bradford (GD)

Pink

Springtime (G)	Louise Gable (G)	Sagittarius (GD)
Eleanor Allan (K)	Rosebud (G)	Cameo (G)
Guy Yerkes (K)	Grace Freeman (GD)	Crinoline (GD)
Eureka (K)	Aphrodite (GD)	

Violet-Purple

Amoenum (K)	Zulu (GD)	Sarabande (GD)
Herbert (G)	Muscadine (GD)	Chanticleer (GD)
Sherwoodi (K)	Purple Splendor (G)	Dauntless (GD)
R. poukanense		

EVERGREEN AZALEAS FOR ZONE 7b to 8a

White

Snow (K)	Delaware Valley White (M)	Gumpo (S)
H. H. Hume (K)	Glacier (GD)	Everest (GD)
Polar Bear (K)	Helen Close (GD)	Swansong (GD)
Mizu-no-yamakuki (K)	Treasure (GD)	Wavelet (GD)

White (Variegated, striped, bordered)

Geisha (GD)	Martha Hitchcock (GD)	Kinghetsu (S)
Ruth May (K)	George Lindley Taber (SI)	Gyokushin (S)
Appleblossom (Ho-o) (K)	Surprise (GD)	Gunrei (S)
Refrain (GD)		Ho-raku (S)

Orange Red–Orange Pink

Coral Bells (Kirin) (K)	Greeting (GD)	Flame Creeper (I)
Bridesmaid (K)	Fashion (GD)	Balsaminaeflorum (I)
Orange Cup (K)	Buccaneer (GD)	Beni-kirin (S)
Salmon Beauty (K)	Lawsal (SI)	Margaret Douglas (BA)
Sherwood Red (K)		

Rose Red

Hino-crimson (K)	Glamour (GD)	Mai-hime (S)
Sherwood Red (K)	Target (BA)	Pearl Bradford (GD)
Christmas Cheer (K)	Hampton Beauty (P)	Macrantha (S)
Hexe (K)		
Hinode-giri (K)		

Pink

Allure (GD)	Aphrodite (GD)	Sagittarius (GD)
Eureka (K)	Grace Freeman (GD)	Waka-bisu (S)
Eleanor Allan (K)	Dawn (P)	Pink Gumpo (S)
Pink Pearl		
(Azuma-Kagami) (K)		Mai-hime (S)
Glory (K)		

Violet–Violet Red

Sherwoodi (K)	Formosa (SI)	Sarabande (GD)
Herbert (G)	Muscadine (GD)	Chanticleer (GD)
Iro-hayama (K)	Purple Splendor (G)	Dauntless (GD)
Koromo-shikibu (K)		

EVERGREEN AZALEAS FOR ZONE 8b to 9

White
Sun Valley (R)	Alaska (R)	Moonbeam (GD)
Snow (K)	Fielder's White (SI)	White Jade (BA)
Gardenia Supreme (P)	Alba Maculata (SI)	Gumpo (S)
H. H. Hume (K)	Mrs. G. G. Gerbing (SI)	Everest (GD)
	Treasure (GD)	

White (Variegated or flecked)
Eastern Parade (R)	Iveryana (SI)	Fawn (GD)
Geisha (GD)	Criterion (SI)	Shinnyo-no-tsuki (S)
Ruth May (K)	George Lindley Taber (SI)	Gyokushin (S)
	Mme. Dominique Vervaene (SI)	Kinghetsu (S)

Orange Red–Orange Pink
Sherwood Red (K)	President Claeys (SI)	Okina-nishiki (I)
Wildfire (GD)	Lawsal (SI)	Eros (GD)
Salmon Beauty (K)	Prince of Orange (SI)	Target (BA)
Coral Bell (Ho-o) (K)	Dorothy Gish (R)	Pat Craft (BA)
	Fashion (GD)	

Rose Red
Christmas Cheer (K)	Giant Ruffles (SI)	Cremona (GD)
Hexe (K)	Redwings (R)	Mai-hime (S)
Hino-crimson (K)	Pride of Dorking (SI)	Pearl Bradford (GD)
Hinode-giri (K)	Watermelon Red (SI)	

Pink
Hampton Beauty (P)	Pride of Mobile (Elegans Superba) (SI)	Sterling (GD)
Sweetheart Supreme (P)	Judge Solomon (SI)	Debonaire (BA)
Allure (GD)	Sweetheart Supreme (P)	Marian Lee (BA)
Glory (K)	Fisher Pink (SI)	Waka-bisu (S)

Violet–Violet Red
Sherwoodi (K)	Formosa (SI)	Sarabande (GD)
Herbert (G)	Omurasaki (SI)	Hexe de Saffelacre (BH)
	Gulf Pride (SI)	Chanticleer (GD)

EVERGREEN AZALEAS FOR ZONE 9a to 9b

The list of azaleas for the deep South was compiled by Dr. Sigmond L. Solymosy, Professor of Horticulture, University of Southwestern Louisiana, Lafayette, Louisiana. He stated "the most difficult question in selecting azaleas for the deep South is the determination of what is early, midseason and late. Are the December-January blooming ones the lates or the earlys; is the October blooming midseason or late compared to the December-January ones?" Many azaleas are inconsistent in their blooming and growth habits in the deep South.

White
Snow (K)	George Lindley Taber (SI)	King's White (R)
H. H. Hume (K)	Mrs. G. G. Gerbing (SI)	Indica Alba
		(R. mucronatum)
Gardenia Supreme (P)	Delaware Valley White (M)	Mary Helen (GD)

White (Variegated, striped and bordered)
Martha Hitchcock (GD)	Mardi Gras (I)	Kinghetsu (S)
Refrain (GD)	Boldface (GD)	Masquerade (GD)
Criterion (SI)	Gyokushin (S)	

Orange Red–Orange Pink
Coral Bells (Kirin) (K)	Greeting (GD)	Copperman (GD)
Glory (K)	Pericat Salmon (P)	Ho-raku (S)
Mme. Joseph Vervaene (BH)	Buccaneer (GD)	Orange Cup (K)

Rose Red
Hinode-giri (K)	Pride of Mobile	
	(Elegans Superba) (SI)	President Claeys (SI)
Pink Pearl		
(Azuma-kagami) (K)	Judge Solomon (SI)	Waka-bisu (S)
Glamour (GD)	Fisher Pink (SI)	Abbot (GD)
	Triomphe de Ledeberg (SI)	

Pink
Sweetheart Supreme (P)	Salmon Solomon (SI)	Janet Noyes (GD)
Grace Freeman (GD)	Pink Ruffles (BH)	Jubilee (GD)
Aphrodite (GD)	Prince of Orange (SI)	Pink Formosa (SI)

Violet–Violet Red
Sherwoodi (K)	Violaces Rubra (SI)	Dixie Beauty (SI)
Gulf Pride (SI)	Formosa (SI)	Meteor (GD)
Glee (GD)	Commando (GD)	

Azalea Gardens — U.S.A.

The colorful flowering azaleas grace Southern highways and parks, formal gardens, neighborhood yards, wooded trails, and narrow mountain roads. Their white, yellow, pink, red, and purple blossoms herald spring with a special brilliance.

In turn, our Southern cities salute the azalea with elaborate seasonal events and specially designed areas.

The peak blooming period for azaleas starts in January and February in Florida, Texas and along the Gulf Coast and continues into May and June in the Virginia and North Carolina mountains. To follow the "azalea trails" as they reach full brilliance in each region would require months of travel. Fortunately, the weekend gardener is not far from a site of multicolored azalea brilliance. With advance planning, he can visit a special azalea trail, a festival, or a formal garden within a short distance from his home.

Many Southern cities and towns proudly display their azaleas in public gardens, on trails, and at special festivals. Our universities and colleges beautify their campuses with azaleas, and many conduct research, plan test areas, and botanical gardens for these plants.

Visiting gardens is an excellent relaxing pastime which can also be of educational value for the gardener. A note book and camera is a must to record the varieties, color combinations, and garden design. Do not adopt ideas or scenes, but rather, learn to adapt ideas for your own garden.

Here are some ideal stops to make while traveling on the azalea trails across the South.

Florida is noted for its exquisite gardens and many are filled with azalea beauty from early January through March.

Cypress Gardens, Winter Haven, Florida, grows azaleas amidst rare and tropical plants from throughout the world.

Sunken Gardens in St. Petersburg, Florida, features azaleas and many exotic semitropical plants in a setting of tall and stately palms.

Ravine Gardens in Palatka, about 50 miles south of Jacksonville, is an 85-acre natural garden. Azaleas are used in a rustic setting along a natural ravine. An Azalea Festival and an Azalea Ball are held annually.

Alfred B. Maclay Gardens State Park (formerly Killearn Gardens) is located five miles north of Tallahassee. The gardens are an outstanding azalea beauty spot, featuring both formal and informal landscaping. The gardens are open daily from September to June; the adjoining picnic area is open year-round.

Information on Florida azaleas, gardens, and festivals is available from the Florida Development Commission Tourist Division, Tallahassee, Florida.

Texas The major cities, such as Dallas and others, feature azaleas in their park plantings. The River Oaks Garden Club of Houston and the City of Tyler annually hold azalea trails. The Big Thicket, a lush wooded region of East Texas is known for its profusion of native azaleas. Several highways (routes) offer the traveler views of the Big Thicket, a deep tangled woods traversing about half a million acres in all, and part of eight East Texas counties from Tyler south to Harden and Polk Counties, near Beaumont, Texas. For additional information on gardens, contact the Texas Tourist Bureau of Austin, Texas.

Louisiana is known for its magnificent mansions and beautiful gardens and one is afraid to list them for fear of overlooking some.

Afton Villa Gardens, near Bains, Louisiana, north of St. Francisville, is a sunken garden with seven terraces, and is laced with century old azaleas.

Rosedown Plantation and Gardens, St. Francisville, is inspiring with enormous camellias and azaleas.

Hodges Gardens, between Many and Leesville, is noted for its extensive planting of cultivated and native azaleas, and is referred to as a garden in the forest.

Rip Van Winkle Gardens, near Belcambre, is an English Garden in a tropical setting.

University of Southwestern Louisana, at Lafayette, is an excellent example of a landscaped college, using both the native and introduced plant materials.

Longue Vue Gardens is a large city estate garden, featuring plants and moving water, located just a few minutes from downtown New Orleans. New Orleans is noted for its beautiful gardens, and a tour of the garden district should be included, in addition to visiting Vieux Carre, the French Quarter, and its enclosed gardens. Shreveport and Baton Rouge are noted for their beautiful gardens, and, while in Shreveport, one should visit the Centenary College campus which features four acres of rolling hills, covered with azaleas.

Information and brochures on Louisiana's gardens are available from the Louisiana Tourist Development Commission, Box 4291, Capitol Station, Baton Rouge, Louisiana 70804.

Arkansas is noted for its abundance of native azaleas. The Ozark Society, a statewide canoeing and conservation club, sponsors a spring azalea bus tour to the native azalea fields in the Ozark Mountains around Clinton.

Information on the tour and dates is available from Dr. Neil Compton, Box 209, Bentonville, Arkansas 72712.

Information on gardens in Arkansas is available from the Arkansas Tourist Bureau, Little Rock, Arkansas.

Mississippi, The gardens of many historic Mississippi homes come alive with azaleas in the spring when special pilgrimage events are held in the cities of Natchez, Vicksburg, Holly Springs, Jackson, Columbus, and in the cities on the Mississippi Gulf Coast. In Jackson, the Mynella Gardens features thousands of azaleas and other plants along a rustic path.

Information on the Mississippi pilgrimages and Mynella Gardens is available from Mississippi Hospitality, 1504 State Office Building, Jackson, Mississippi 39201.

Alabama. Mobile is famous for its annual Azalea Trail in the early spring. The trail is part of the city's Mardi Gras and a highlight of the azalea festival is the pageant to select America's Junior Miss. Information on the exact dates and events is available from the Mobile Chamber of Commerce, Government Street, Mobile, Alabama.

Bellingrath Gardens, south of Mobile near Theodore, features thousands of azaleas and camellias among the moss-hung oaks. In Long's Garden, in Mobile, beautiful pine knolls and landscaped ravines are covered with azaleas. Clarke Gardens, also in Mobile, features azaleas and other plants in a charming rural setting. Birmingham Botanical Gardens is developing a rhododendron and azalea garden.

Montgomery, Auburn, and Birmingham have garden tours in the spring.

Information and brochures are available from

the Bureau of Publicity and Information, State Capitol, Montgomery, Alabama 36104.

Georgia. Best known for azaleas in Georgia is Callaway Gardens at Pine Mountain. Native azaleas color the hillsides and trails through the 2,500 acre pine and hardwood sanctuary. The Azalea Trail is over 1½ miles in length and features over 600 different species and cultivars of azaleas. The peak of the azalea season is early to mid-April, however, many plants are still in flower until August. Information is available from Callaway Gardens.

Savannah is noted for its lovely gardens where azaleas bloom. Forsyth Park and Bonaventure Cemetery have profusions of azaleas shaded by moss covered oaks. Wormsloe Plantation and Gardens on the Isle of Hope, south of Savannah, is alive with the color of azaleas each spring. Write to the Savannah Chamber of Commerce, Box 530, Savannah, Georgia 31402, for flowering dates and information on the gardens.

Atlanta is spectacular when azaleas and dogwoods are in bloom, and it is billed as the "Dogwood City of the South". Maps for self-guided tours of the azalea-dogwood sites and information on the dogwood festival are available from the Women's Chamber of Commerce of Atlanta, 1101 Commerce Building, Atlanta, Georgia 30303.

Thomasville is noted for its azalea displays in early March. The city streets, parks, and private gardens combine to make an outstanding display, which when combined with camellias, wild crabapple, and dogwood make an outstanding festival of color. But, gardeners in that city quickly put aside thoughts of azaleas and camellias to make way for the rose festival in April! The Chamber of Commerce can advise specific information for a visit to this horticulturally minded city. Augusta, Macon, and Columbus are also noted

for their azaleas and garden tours. Information is available from their Chamber of Commerce.

South Carolina is noted, from the coast to the highlands, for its outstanding displays of azaleas.

Kalmia Gardens, west of Hartsville, displays masses of azaleas and other plants of the low country.

Boone Hall Plantation and Gardens at Mount Pleasant features exquisite azaleas planted in a formal plantation setting amid garden walls and buildings dating from the 1600's.

Edesto Gardens near Orangeburg display azaleas in the shade of moss hung trees.

Belle Isle, a former 5,000 acre rice plantation at Georgetown, is brilliant with azaleas each spring.

Brookgreen Gardens north of Georgetown is noted for its magnificent collection of sculpture features native azaleas and other indigenous plants.

Charleston, a city famous for flowers, is noted for three elegant gardens.

Magnolia Gardens, a great river plantation paradise just northwest of Charleston, is famed for its large variety and profusion of azaleas growing beneath draped cypresses in quiet river inlets.

Middletown Gardens, also northwest of Charleston, are the oldest landscaped gardens in America, and feature brilliant masses of azaleas and other plants.

Cypress Gardens, north of Charleston, is noted for its black lagoons through old gnarled cypress groves and the banks of the lagoons glow with azaleas.

Information on South Carolina's azalea gardens and trails is available from the State Development Board, Columbia, South Carolina.

North Carolina. Wilmington is noted for its annual Azalea Festival and azalea displays. The festival program includes garden tours, art displays, and a coronation pageant for the azalea queen. Information is available from Azalea Festival, P.O. Box 51, Wilmington, North Carolina 28401.

Azalea Gardens throughout the state include:

Greenfield Park in Wilmington offers a 5 mile drive around a lake lined with azaleas.

Orton Plantation south of Wilmington has formal gardens colored by extensive plantings of azaleas. Airlie Gardens in Wilmington also features azaleas. Clarendon Gardens near Southern Pines features numerous azaleas and many other plants.

Biltmore Gardens at the Biltmore Estate in Asheville includes a large collection of native azaleas and other indigenous plants.

The Ashville Botanical Garden features native plants and has a good collection of native azaleas. Duke Gardens at Duke University in Durham features azaleas and other colorful plants for its students and visitors.

North Carolina State University at Raleigh, North Carolina, has an interesting ornamental test garden including azaleas. The University of North Carolina at Charlotte has a rhododendron test garden with a wooded site on the campus.

Native azaleas are plentiful in the North Carolina mountains, particularly on Grandfather Mountain, Wayah Bald, and along the Blue Ridge Parkway north of Asheville,

southwest through Mount Pisgah to the Great Smoky Mountains National Park. Craggy Gardens north of Ashville on the Blue Ridge Parkway is noted for its display of rhododendrons in June.

Information and booklets on North Carolina's gardens is available from the Travel Information Division, Dept. of Conservation and Development, Raleigh, North Carolina.

Tennessee. The Memphis Botanical Garden features cultivated azaleas in an informal planting under large hardwood trees.

Cheekwood, the Nashville Botanical Gardens, has added a new azalea garden to its lovely setting. Knoxville and Chattanooga are both noted for their lovely gardens and garden tours.

Flame azaleas provide brilliant color in the Great Smoky Mountains. The best azalea display is on Gregory Bald in the Cades Cove area. A mountain trail of approximately 9 miles is strenuous, but well worth the struggle for the mountain high display. Andrews Bald is available by a shorter walk of approximately 4 miles for another azalea site. The azaleas on Gregory Bald are usually in flower in late June.

Roan Mountain south of Elizabethton is noted for its display of Catawba rhododendrons on a high grassy bald.

Information on gardens in Tennessee is available from the Travel Bureau in Nashville, Tennessee.

Virginia. Azaleas bloom in profusion along the wooded trails in Norfolk's Garden-By-The-Sea. A highlight of the azalea season is Norfolk's International Azalea Festival each April. Information on the azalea festival is available from the Norfolk Chamber of Commerce, 262 Boush Street, Norfolk,

Virginia 23510.

Richmond has several parks featuring azaleas. Bryan Park of 250 acres is spectacular in the spring with many thousands of azaleas. Maymount Park, once a famous Richmond estate, features, in addition to azaleas, Japanese and Italian gardens.

Spring is also azalea time in the Shenandoah National Park in the heart of the Blue Ridge Mountains. Along the 105 mile Skyline Drive azaleas bloom in late spring from the valley floor to the crest of the Blue Ridge.

Information on the Parkway is available from the National Park Service of the United States Department of the Interior. Information on Virginia's gardens is available from the Department of Conservation and Economic Development, Richmond, Virginia.

The National Arboretum in Washington, D. C., is noted for its excellent collection of azaleas on Hamilton Hill. The Morrison Garden featuring Glenn Dale azaleas and Fred Lee Garden of Satsuki azaleas add to the azalea collection. Numerous other plants are featured at the Arboretum.

Azalea and rhododendron enthusiasts are urged to join the American Rhododendron Society. The Society has 37 chapters throughout the country that hold monthly or quarterly meetings. The Society publishes an excellent quarterly with color pictures, holds a national meeting each year, plus many other benefits to members.

For information on the Society and its chapters, write to:
American Rhododendron Society
c/o Executive Secretary, Bernice J. Lamb
2232 N.E. 78th Avenue
Portland, Oregon 91213

The following A.R.S. Chapters are in the South and its center of interest:
Azalea Chapter, Atlanta, Georgia
Birmingham Chapter, Birmingham, Alabama
Middle Atlantic Chapter, Richmond, Virginia
Piedmont Chapter, Asheville, North Carolina
Southeastern Chapter, Charlotte, North Carolina
Southern Chapter, Texas
Tidewater Chapter, Norfolk, Virginia

Glossary

Aeration
Exposing to the circulation of air for purification.

Air Layering
A method of plant propagation which is accomplished on the parent plant.

Appressed
Pressed close to or lying flat against something.

Azalea
Any of a group of deciduous or evergreen shrubs, part of the genus *Rhododendron*, of the North Temperate Zone, many of which are cultivated for their showy, variously colored flowers.

Bagasse
Residue of sugarcane after the juice has been extracted.

Botanist
One who specializes in the study of plants.

Botany
The science of plants; the branch of biology dealing with plant life.

Cambium
A thin layer of tissue under the bark, consisting of cells capable of dividing themselves and forming new layers of wood, bark, or other tissue.

Chlorosis
A diseased condition in chlorophyll-bearing plants manifested as yellowing or blanching of the normally green parts due to causes other than the absence of light, such as attacks by parasites or mineral deficiencies such as an iron deficiency.

Clone
A group of plants derived by vegetative propagation from one original plant.

Conifer
Cone-bearing trees, such as pines, firs, and spruces.

Corolla
The petals of a flower, collectively.

Cultivar
A group of individuals within a species which are distinct in form or function from other similar individuals. Commonly referred to as a variety.

Cultivate
To loosen or break up the soil for the purpose of killing weeds and modifying moisture retention of the soil.

Cuttings
The parts of a plant used to start new plants—usually the stems, leaves, or roots.

Cycad
A palm-like tropical plant.

Damping Off
A diseased condition of seedlings or cuttings caused by certain parasitic fungi that invade the plant tissues near the ground and produce wilting usually associated with rotting of the stem especially near the ground level.

Deciduous
Leaf-losing, not ever-green.

Defoliation
May be caused by disease, insects, or too much or too little moisture.

Dimorphic
Occurring in two forms.

Division
The process of starting new plants by removing a portion of a plant—usually the roots, shoots, or above-ground sections.

Dwarf
An atypically small animal or plant. To check the natural growth or development of.

Evergreen
Having foliage that persists and remains green throughout the year.

Foliar Fertilizing
Fertilizing plants by spraying on them nutrient solutions to be absorbed by the foliage.

Forcing
Modifying temperatures or other environmental conditions to cause the production of flowers earlier or later than their normal seasons.

Friable
Easily crumbled, pulverized, or reduced to powder.

Fungicide
A chemical used to kill or reduce the growth of fungus organisms that cause disease.

Fungus
A group of lower plants lacking chlorophyll, including molds, rusts, mildews, smuts, etc.

Gall
A swelling on the tissues of plants caused by insects, fungi, or other organisms.

Genus
A taxonomic category ranking below a family and above a species. A class of individuals divided into subordinate species having certain common attributes.

Glabrous
Not hairy or pubescent.

Glandular
Bearing glands or gland-like appendages or protuberance.

Glaucous
Having a blue-green waxy surface.

Graft
To unite a shoot or bud with a growing plant by insertion or placing in close contact.

Harden Off
To prepare a plant for colder or more rigorous conditions by gradually raising or lowering temperatures, or by withholding water so that the plant can be transferred from indoors to outdoors.

Hardiness
Ability of a plant to withstand winter outdoors in a cold climate without protection.

Head Back
To prune severely main branches or rapidly growing shoots.

Heel In
To plant close together temporarily.

Herbaceous
Refers to seed-bearing plants that die to the ground each year, commonly used when describing perennials.

High-Analysis Fertilizer
A fertilizer which contains high proportions of nutrient elements ($N-P_2O-K_2$) as found in a 10-10-10 or 20-20-20 formula.

Hose-in-hose
Flowers appear to have two cycles of petals, one growing within the other so that the calyx and corolla look alike.

Humus
Material formed by the partial decomposition of vegetable or animal matter; the organic portion of soil.

Hybrid
A crossbreed between two different species or inbred lines within a species.

Inflorescence
A complete flower cluster.

Inorganic Fertilizer
A fertilizer that does not contain carbon compounds.

Insecticide
A material used for the control or eradication of insects.

Layering
To propagate by layering, that is, to bend down a shoot and cover with soil for propagation.

Leaching
To remove soluble constituents from a substance by the action of a liquid.

Leaf Mold
Compost formed of leaves.

Lepidote Scales
Small scurfy scales usually on the underside of a leaf.

Lifting
Digging up and removing a plant from the soil.

Loam
Soil consisting of clay, sand, and organic materials in varying proportions.

Microclimate
The climate of a small area which differs from that of the general surrounding region because of special conditions.

Mulch

A substance, such as straw, which is spread over the ground to protect the roots of plants.

Mutation

A fundamental change in heredity that produces a new plant basically unlike the parent, or that produces part of a plant that differs significantly from the main body.

Mycorrhiza

A soil fungi associated with the roots of ericaceous plants that aids the roots in the absorption of nutrients and water in a mutual or symbiotic relationship.

Naturalize

To establish plants as if they grew by chance so that they persist with a minimum of care.

Natural Layering

The spontaneous rooting of stems in contact with the ground.

Nematode

One of a group of tiny worm-like creatures that damage plants by feeding on or within the roots.

Nitrates

Certain salts or nitric acid, which are used as oxidizing agents in the manufacturing of fertilizers.

Nonglandular

Without glands.

Overwinter

To provide conditions so that plants can live through the winter.

Organic Fertilizer

A fertilizer containing carbon compounds.

Peat Moss (Sphagnum Moss)

Coarse, fibrous material which has not decayed.

Peat (Mulch)

Well rotted, organic matter composed of fine particles.

Perlite

Lightweight expanded mineral kernels frequently used in combination with peat moss as a rooting medium.

Pesticide

Any chemical or mixture of chemicals used to control plant and animal pests including insects, diseases, weeds, rodents, etc.

pH

Symbol used to express the degree of acidity or alkalinity. pH 7.0 is neutral, below 7.0 is acid, and above is alkaline.

Pinch Back

The removing of the soft tip of a shoot, usually with the fingers, to induce branching.

Pollen

The mass of dust-like grains (male reproduction cells) in seed plants.

Pollination

The transfer of pollen from the stamen of a plant to the stigma of another.

Prepare Soil

Break or turn soil or sod to a depth of 6 to 8 inches, breaking up clods and/or mixing in fertilizer and crop residues or adding peat or compost.

Propagation

To start new plants from seed, cuttings, or other plant parts.

Prune

To cut off or cut back parts of a plant for better shape or for more fruitful growth.

Pubescence

A covering of soft short hairs.

Pubescent

Covered with short, soft hairs.

Rhododendron

Any of various evergreen shrubs of the genus *Rhododendron*, of the North Temperate Zone, having clusters of variously colored flowers.

Rooting Media

Any ingredient or combination of ingredients which will provide a well-aerated, well-drained, yet moisture retentive environment for rooting cuttings. The safest medium is one that contains only sterile ingredients.

Rootstock

The root or stem and roots of the plant to

which a scion is joined for grafting or budding.

Runner

A slender stem which grows along the top of the ground and bears young plants.

Seedling

A young plant grown from seeds as distinguished from one propagated by a vegetative post such as a cutting.

Set

A young bulb or tuber which is ready for planting.

Scion

The stem of the plant that is to be joined with the root stock of another plant during grafting.

Species

A class of individuals grouped by virtue of their common attributes and assigned a common name; a division subordinate to a genus.

Sport

Mutation.

Stamen

The male organ of a flower.

Stoloniferous

A plant producing runner or any basal branch that is inclined to root and give rise to a new plant.

Sucker

A shoot of a bush or tree that arises from below ground level rather than from the stem or trunk.

Symbiosis

The intimate living together of two dissimilar organisms in any of various mutually beneficial relationships, as in parasitism and mutalism.

Taxonomist

A specialist in taxonomy or the orderly classification of plants and animals according to their presumed natural relationships.

Taxonomy

The theory, principles, and process of classifying organisms in established categories.

Tender Plant

A plant that cannot survive freezing temperatures.

Trace Elements

Chemical elements needed by plants only in minute quantities (also known as micronutrients).

Transplant

To lift and reset a plant in another soil or situation.

Understock

The root system and base stem of plants upon which other plants are grafted.

Variety (or Cultivar)

The subdivision of a species. A group of individuals within a species which are distinct in form or function from other similar individuals. Also known as cultivar.

Index